HAWAIIAN

✹ ✹ ✹ ✹ ✹

COUNTRY TABLES

Vintage Recipes for Today's Cook

Kaui Philpotts

THE
BESS
PRESS

3565 Harding Ave. Honolulu, Hawai'i 96816 (808) 734-7159 fax (808) 732-3627 www. besspress. com

Design: Carol Colbath

Philpotts, Kaui
    Hawaiian country tables : vintage recipes
for today's cook / Kaui Philpotts
        p.   cm.
    Includes illustrations, glossary, index.
ISBN 1-57306-076-3

Printed in Korea

TABLE OF **C**ONTENTS

Acknowledgments

I owe all my friends and relatives for their good humor and good cooking. It was the missing of them and the old times growing up on Pāʻia plantation that really inspired this book. There is no more plantation camp, so there's no going home, except through food and memories.

I thank my father, Pete St. Sure, for instilling in me a passion for local cooking, and our family and friends for keeping it alive. If my editor at *The Maui News*, Nora Cooker, had never given me a chance to do the food pages that no one else wanted, I would never have discovered how much I love writing about food.

My buddies Lynne Horner, Carol Hartley, and Carol Austin have listened to me talk about this book endlessly and deserve my thanks for their patience and affection.

Mahalo to Maili Yardley, the Maui Cooks, and all the unsung home cooks who've contributed to the numerous community cookbooks I've collected through the years. And to Tutu, Robbie, Charlie, Dani, Woozer, Stewart, and Joelle for eating what I served up.

And of course, to my husband, Dougie Philpotts, who thinks I'm a much better cook and writer than I am.

Introduction

The seed for this book was planted thirty years ago when, homesick and very young, I tried to recreate a dish from my childhood on a hot plate in a rundown walk-up in San Francisco's North Beach—for an artist I was trying to impress. It was a simple beef-tomato stir-fry. I knew what it should taste like, but I didn't know exactly how to prepare it.

In the years that followed, as a wife and mother, feature writer and food editor, I became aware of how special the dishes made by the Islands' ethnically diverse home cooks really were. At just about any gathering, the table is set with foods from Japan, China, Korea, the Philippines, the mainland United States, and Hawai'i. Over the generations since their first arrival, these foods have changed and evolved into something uniquely Hawaiian in character.

Island "Stew"

My own family is a perfect example of this island "stew" created over generations of intermarriage and cultural sharing. My paternal Grandmother St. Sure was the daughter of an Ojibway Indian from White Earth, Minnesota, brought around "the horn" to Hawai'i in the 1860s by missionaries invited by King Kamehameha IV to establish an Episcopal church on the island of Maui.

I remember Grandmother St. Sure as a haughty, strong, opinionated woman used to getting her way. Even in her later years, her table was always perfectly set, as it must have been when her children were growing up and she had live-in household help. She never entertained anymore, but the table sat there with its silver and its glass goblets, ready at a moment's notice to feed six for lunch.

I'm not really sure Grandmother St. Sure even knew how to cook. She did do one thing well—popovers. Light and airy and perfectly browned. As teenagers watching our weight, my cousins and I would refuse to eat them. But she'd insist. "They're nothing. Just a bit of air," she'd say.

My father was Grandmother St. Sure's fifth and last child. By the time he came along she'd lost all interest in raising children and delegated the job to a Japanese couple who worked for her and lived in tiny quarters behind the house near the vegetable garden.

From them my father learned to cook "island style" food. He cooked nothing else until the day he died. My father had a passion for cooking. In those "white bread" days of the 1950s, our refrigerator was filled with jars of dau see (Chinese black bean sauce), whole star anise, and threads of mysterious oriental seasonings. My father cooked every single family meal and never allowed any of us in his kitchen (my mother was banished to yard duty, which she preferred anyway). He was a culinary tyrant.

His concern for his perfectly maintained set of knives bordered on hysteria. "Who touched my knives!" he'd scream upon coming home from his desk job at the sugar plantation to find we'd used one of them on a ripe mango and then left the whole mess—peel, seed, and runny juice—in the sink.

Granny Shaw, my maternal grandmother, was perhaps at the opposite end of the spectrum. She was the daughter of a Hawaiian-Chinese woman, so sweet she was destined for sainthood, and a rambunctious, red-headed Scotsman who came to Hawai'i to work as a luna (supervisor) on a Big Island sugar plantation in the mid-1800s. Granny Shaw's grandfather, called either Aiko (by Hawaiians) or Lum Jo, had come to the islands from Canton, China, earlier in that century to operate a small sugar mill in the Kohala district of the island of Hawai'i in the days before sugar became "king."

Granny Shaw was a downhome cook. She walked to the fish market every morning for reef fish like akule and mullet—local fish I often find too much trouble to prepare today (too strong in flavor and with too many bones). She would cut the fish into large pieces and salt it before placing it on a wooden frame between wire netting to dry in the sun.

On the days she wasn't inclined to cook lunch, she'd pull a bowl of souring poi (mashed taro), covered with what I always thought was a shower cap, out of the refrigerator. We'd eat the poi and the dried fish with chunks of sweet onions she'd pickled in vinegar and chili pepper. Sometimes there would be small dishes of leftovers from the night before. Hamburger boiled with tomatoes and seasonings, green beans with bits of pork in a soy sauce. It was a feast.

This book is an attempt to keep alive the memories of Hawai'i's country tables in the days before Burger King and McDonald's. Before we were absorbed into the homogenized union of the United States. Before chic young chefs created a new regional cuisine for stylish restaurants.

ISLAND HOSPITALITY

I have always been charmed by the graciousness of island hospitality exhibited during the 1930s, 1940s, and 1950s. Admittedly, much of my vision is purely romantic. Still, it persists. As in the American South, houseguests and relatives were entertained royally because they visited rarely. When they made the trip to one of Hawai'i's neighbor islands—to a beach house at Kapoho or an Upcountry ranch on the slopes of Haleakalā or Hualālai—they usually stayed awhile.

Produce and ingredients for meals came from backyards or a next-door neighbor's. The dishes people came up with were much more closely connected to what was in the backyard than today—foods like taro biscuits and Surinam cherry and starfruit jam.

Today much of that great backyard produce, those jams and jellies, breads and spice mixes, can be found only in church and community bazaars and weekend flea markets. Most young people no longer know how to make them—even if they had the time.

I live a busy life and so do you. Yet, we still receive gifts from neighbor's trees and gardens—avocados, cherimoya, blood oranges, loquat, and bananas. And more often than not, we don't know what to do with the bounty. This book will provide you with ideas.

THE RECIPES

Many of the original recipes are taken from my collection of old community cookbooks, adapted to contemporary tastes wherever possible. Although it is now the fashion to write recipes using reduced-calorie and reduced-fat ingredients. I have not done so here, as I believe old recipes should stick as closely to the original ingredients as possible to maintain the integrity of their flavor. If you have special dietary concerns, in most cases reduced-calorie margarine can be substituted for butter, lite shoyu for regular strength, reduced-fat mayonnaise for regular, and so on.

In most of the recipes I have used whole ingredients rather than mixes or other prepared-food shortcuts, simply because I believe they are better for you. However, if you are rushing, or do not have the ingredients on hand, there is nothing wrong with substituting instant for "made from scratch" or using frozen in place of fresh. In a pinch, we all use conveniences such as prepared pie crust or canned chicken broth.

This book is meant to be used by a home cook of average ability, with a romantic heart and a yen for adventure. In writing it, I have tried to preserve some of the past with its rich, cultural heritage from both the East and West. It is an attempt to share the culinary traditions of this special part of the world. It is a celebration of our differences and our common humanity.

The Basics

The two foods at the very heart of the Native Hawaiian diet were poi and salt. To those two items Hawaiians could add anything they wished—fish, taro leaves, pork—and have a meal. This section describes those and other staples, with tips on preparing and using them.

Traditional Poi

Jokes about the resemblance between poi and wallpaper paste are commonplace after years of visitor industry lū'au. Yet Hawaiians raised on poi-sugar-and-milk cocktails since birth love it with all their heart. Admittedly, it's an acquired taste, but its praises have been sung for years by doctors trying to feed finicky babies allergic to other foods.

Poi is a starchy, sticky paste made from pounding the corm of the taro plant with water until it reaches a smooth consistency. It's rare to find anyone today who makes poi at home "from scratch." Instead, poi is purchased in markets (which have acquired it from small poi factories) ready to be thinned to a desired consistency.

Native Hawaiians practiced an etiquette when eating poi that has almost been forgotten. It was, for instance, eaten with one or two fingers of the hand (never three). The fingers were rotated several times in the bowl, and whatever clung to them was lifted to the mouth. It was considered very bad manners to scoop poi from the bowl, or to drag poi across the bowl and up into the mouth.

Discussing business over an open bowl of poi was considered bad luck, and the scolding of children or discussion of unpleasant subjects was avoided. On the other hand, it was considered good manners to smack your lips in approval.

While traditional poi is still popular at lū'au and in Hawaiian restaurants and homes, many contemporary cooks are more likely to use it in muffins, biscuits, or pancakes. Poi is available frozen or bottled for use on the mainland. There is also a commercial brand of taro flour baking mix that is handy.

Native Hawaiians made poi from breadfruit (poi ʻulu), sweet potato (poi ʻuala), and potato starch, in addition to taro.

The easiest way to prepare packaged poi is to pour about half a cup of water into the opened plastic bag, then reseal it and knead the poi and water together until it softens and separates from the bag. That way you can mix it to the thickness you like and keep your hands clean. Add water slowly. Too much water at once will leave the poi lumpy, so work it in a little at a time.

When the poi has been mixed, place it in a bowl and pour a thin layer of tap water over the top to avoid having it dry out when refrigerated. Cover the bowl with plastic wrap.

In the old days, when there was no refrigeration, poi was kept in calabashes. To this day, many Hawaiians love "sour poi" (poi that is not freshly made). After the arrival of Westerners, they often kept poi in a kelemānia, or German crock, also used for sauerkraut and pickles.

MAKING CHILI PEPPER WATER

Bottled homemade chili pepper water has long been a staple on island home tables. More recently it has appeared on stylish bistro tables as well. Several Hawaiian regional chefs have come out with their own commercial versions, which while slightly more complex, are still in the spirit of the original.

Small, red Hawaiian chili peppers are added to plain white vinegar and garlic, then puréed and left to "age" for a few weeks before being used as a seasoning (see recipe, page 117). The Asian-influenced version includes sugar, shoyu (soy sauce), ginger, and sesame oil. The chili pepper water should be refrigerated and shaken before use. It can be used to season anything from a bowl of noodles to grilled fish or meat.

HAWAIIAN SALT

Hawaiian salt is a coarse sea salt gathered at the water's edge after a storm or high tide. It's most often plentiful during the summer months, because the weather is hotter and the days longer. During the winter months, storms push seawater into tidal holes, where the sun dries out the crystals. The salt is then gathered gingerly and put into burlap bags to be dried further and stored. When the salt is dry, chunks are broken off and crushed with a poi pounder, the Hawaiian version of a mortar and pestle.

Kosher salt is a good substitute for Hawaiian salt when the latter is not available. Common salt mixes in Hawaiʻi include the coarse variety mixed with either small, fresh chili peppers, raw sugar, coarse peppercorns, garlic, or ginger. Many of these mixes are available commercially.

POKE

Poke is a traditional chopped and seasoned raw fish dish. The word poke literally means "blocks" in Hawaiian, and most likely came about after Hawaiians observed fish being cut up into blocks to be salted and stored by early sailors.

Although restaurant chefs and home cooks are creating new, exciting versions of poke, the most traditional poke is simply raw fish sprinkled with Hawaiian salt, ground kukui (candlenut) nuts, and limu (seaweed). The Asian-influenced variety includes shoyu, chili pepper, garlic, sesame oil, and sesame seeds.

Hawaiians often preferred using a darker-meat fish such as

aku (skipjack tuna) and never wasted any part. They ate the darker portions and left the skin on the fish. Today, more modern tastes prefer 'ahi (yellowfin tuna) and other mild-flavored fish, trimmed of all dark flesh and skin.

PAPAYA

The variety of papaya most often used in Hawai'i is the solo papaya. It is relatively small and fragrant, with a yellow flesh. In other parts of the world, papaya have been known to grow to the size of watermelons and often have a bright pink flesh. All types are suitable for island recipes.

When preparing papaya to be eaten as a breakfast fruit, simply cut off the stem end, cut in half, and seed. Many like it served chilled, with a wedge of lemon or lime.

Papaya is very high in vitamin A and can be eaten raw or cooked. Peel and slice for a fruit salad, or keep the skin on and stuff and bake it like a potato for a totally different taste. Papaya can be made into pickles, sorbets, pie fillings, and jams.

Papaya contains an enzyme that helps us digest protein and is often used to help cure an upset stomach or indigestion or as a meat tenderizer.

LILIKO'I, OR PASSION FRUIT

Liliko'i grows plentifully on a vine and looks like a large, overgrown, yellow plum. The "passion" in passion fruit comes from the fact that its flower resembles a Maltese cross, not from any aphrodisiac qualities in the fruit.

Island chefs most often use liliko'i in its

juice form to make sauces and desserts. It is a natural substitute for lemon juice.

To make the juice, cut the liliko'i in half and spoon the seeds and juice into a sieve placed over a bowl. Press the juice from the seeds through the sieve and toss out the pulp and seeds that are left. The juice can be frozen as is or mixed with one part sugar to five parts juice. Add water to taste for a beverage.

Liliko'i is particularly good in a chiffon pie filling and in sorbet. Thickened and seasoned, it works well as a sauce for fish or poultry.

TI LEAVES—THE PERFECT HAWAIIAN WRAPPING

Smooth, fresh-smelling ti leaves are essential to the Hawaiian kitchen. Old-style houses were often encircled by ti leaves to keep evil spirits away. Ti leaves are used to spiritually cleanse at ceremonies and as a kind of "Hawaiian tin foil" in cooking. They are a mainstay throughout Polynesia.

On the mainland, corn husks, grape leaves, banana leaves, and aluminum foil are good substitutes, but the original ti is still the best, as it imparts a very particular flavor to cooked foods.

Hawaiians also use ti leaves to make hula skirts and leis, packages (pū'olo), and liners for food trays. To prepare a ti leaf for cooking purposes, first remove the rib of the leaf with a sharp knife, starting from the tip. Do not cut the leaf itself. With the rib removed, the leaf will become pliable and can be used to wrap food in packages tied with kitchen string (or the removed rib) and then steamed or baked.

PREPARING MACADAMIA NUTS

It is not likely that you will ever have to gather and husk macadamia nuts for your cooking, since they are so easily available already prepared. However, once the nuts are gathered and husked, this is how you prepare them:

Place the gathered and husked nuts in a basket and hang in a dry place. They can be stored for as long as three weeks to six months before cracking. Roast the nuts in single layers in cake pans for two hours at 150 degrees F. Larger nuts may be left in for up to four hours. Cool.

To crack, place the nut in an indented part of a chopping block (or a crack in a cement walkway) and hit it using a light-weight hammer. The nut will almost always come out whole.

Macadamia nuts may be frozen and used as needed. If stored in a jar, they have a tendency to become rancid.

There are two ways to salt macadamia nuts. The first is to sauté them in butter or oil and lightly salt, then cool and place in an airtight jar. The second way is to soak the nuts in salted water overnight and then dry them in a single layer in a shallow baking pan in the oven for one hour at 150 degrees F.

HOW TO CUT A FRESH PINEAPPLE

Twist or cut the top off the fresh fruit.

Then cut the stem and bottom ends of the pineapple off. Next, slice the tough, prickly outside peel from top to bottom in strips all around the fruit until the yellow core is revealed. Pick out and discard any "eyes." The pineapple can now be cut into wedges or bite-sized pieces. Trim off the core. It's fibrous and not very good eating.

COCONUTS

Puncture one of the "eyes" of a husked coconut with a sharp, pointed tool such as an ice pick. Pour out the coconut water, then crack the coconut by hitting it with a hammer in the middle where the shell is the widest. Continue around the coconut until you have cracked the shell in a circle and can separate the two halves. Some people strain any particles from the coconut water and chill it to drink later. However, it does not keep longer than a day or so. Pry the coconut meat out of the shell with a sharp, heavy knife.

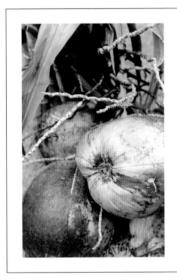

An alternate method is to heat the coconut in a preheated 350 degree F. oven for 15 minutes, then let it sit until it is cool enough to handle. Wrap the coconut in a kitchen towel and crack it into pieces with a hammer.

Shaving coconut: Break the meat into small pieces, peel off the brown outer skin, and then grate the meat with the large holes of a box grater or use a vegetable peeler to make shavings. Coconut may be shredded in a food processor using the shredding disk or chopped finely with the steel blade.

Toasting coconut: To toast fresh coconut, slice the peeled meat thinly with a sharp paring knife. Arrange the slices on a baking sheet and bake in a preheated oven at 300 degrees F. for 15 to 20 minutes, or until golden. To toast dried coconut, reduce the baking time to 5 to 7 minutes.

Making coconut milk: To make fresh coconut milk, place freshly grated coconut in a cheesecloth. Place the cheesecloth bundle in a large pot. Pour boiling hot water over the cheesecloth bundle. When the water and coconut are cool enough to handle, squeeze the coconut milk out through the cheesecloth into the pot. Fresh coconut milk is used in many island recipes. It must be refrigerated immediately or prepared right before use. A sweeter, thicker variety, canned in Thailand, is available in Asian groceries. This can also be used in island dishes.

PREPARING TARO

Whenever you work with taro be sure to wear gloves, or oil your hands and arms, as it contains calcium oxalate crystals, which can irritate your skin.

Peel the outer rough skin of the taro corm and cut the inside meat into large chunks. Place the taro in a pot with enough water to cover. Boil for about 40 minutes, until tender. Some people like to change the water several times during the boiling process. Allow to cool slightly, but not completely. You can now "rice" the taro by forcing it through a strainer or ricer while it is still warm. Do not use a food processor or electric mixer. The riced taro can now be used in muffin and bread recipes or to prepare taro cakes.

PREPARING BREADFRUIT

Breadfruit ('ulu) in modern Hawai'i has gone the way of taro and mangoes. Years ago breadfruit trees, with their lovely leaf patterns, were seen regularly in yards and public spaces. The delicious and nutritious fruit was cooked often and enjoyed.

But in recent years, breadfruit, like taro and mangoes, are harder to find and more mysterious to prepare.

The important thing to remember about breadfruit, if you have access to a tree or if someone nice gives you breadfruit from theirs, is that its flavor (and calorie count) changes as it ripens. Green breadfruit is starchy and needs to be boiled until it is tender. As it gets ripe, it becomes softer and much sweeter. (Perfect for dessert.)

The white sap from the fruit will stain

your clothing permanently. As a precaution, rub your hands with cooking oil and wear junk clothing when working with it. Here is one way to prepare it:

SIMPLE BOILED BREADFRUIT

3 cups water (salted)
4 cups diced green breadfruit
  Salt and pepper to taste
4 tablespoons butter

In a large pot, bring the water to a boil. Add salt and the diced breadfruit that has had the stem, core, and outer skin removed. Boil for about 1 hour, or until tender. Drain and season with salt and pepper and a liberal amount of butter. This can be served in place of rice or potatoes with dinner. Serves 4.

PROCESSING CHUTNEY OR JAM

Sterilize the jars and lids (without the rubber rings) by placing a rack inside a large pot of water and then placing the jars and lids on top. Simmer, do not boil, the equipment uncovered for 10 minutes. You can reuse the jars and rubber rings, but purchase new lids each time you process to insure a safe seal.

Remove the jars with tongs and drain any water. Using a ladle, fill clean, sterilized jars to within 1/4 inch of the top with the chutney (or jam). With a clean towel, wipe any spillage off the jars. Using the tongs, remove the lids from the water and place on jar tops. Screw down the band and lid without forcing.

Place the jars on the rack in the hot-water bath. The jars should not touch the side and should be about an inch away from each other. Cover the pot tightly and bring the water to a boil. Boil for about 10 minutes. Using tongs, lift the jars onto a wire rack to cool. If you are making jam, check the recipe for timing for specific fruits.

In 24 hours, test the seal by pressing the lid. If it doesn't flex up and down, it is properly sealed. (If it does flex, don't worry. You can still eat the chutney, but store it in the refrigerator instead of on the shelf.) Label and store your chutney. Keeps for about 1 year.

1

ʻŌKOLE MALUNA

"Bottoms Up"
Beverages and Appetizers

In Hawaiʻi, it's downright rude to invite someone into your home and not offer something to drink and nibble on. Drinks and pupus, as appetizers are called, have always been an important part of Hawaiian hospitality.

Pupus can be anything from the freshest sashimi and spicy macadamia nuts to pipikaula (beef jerky) and vegetables with kim chee (Korean cabbage pickle) dip. Most often the offering is substantial.

Another island favorite is poke—chunks of fresh fish, usually ʻahi (tuna) or tako (squid) mixed with seaweed, green onion, kukui nut, sesame oil, and chili pepper water. Poke is sold in most local fish markets, and you're as likely to find it in a take-out container on a picnic table, accompanied by a cold beer, as at a fancy cocktail party.

Island appetizers reflect the tastes of all the diverse ethnic groups who have settled here. Some are island "knock-offs" of popular mainland appetizers that substitute typical island ingredients, as in the Macadamia Pesto Cheesecake (see page 18).

9

Carol's Freezer Martinis

Serves 4

There's still nothing like a martini when you're in the mood. While these are not the classic martini, they are very good and can be made ahead and sit in your freezer until you are ready to drink them. They come out almost syrupy.

3 jiggers gin
4 jiggers vodka
2 jiggers water
1 jigger dry vermouth

Mix the ingredients together and place in a jar. Place in the freezer until ready to drink. The martinis should be thoroughly cold. They will become thick, but will not freeze. Pour into chilled martini glasses and garnish with a lemon peel, olive, or onion.

Classic Mai Tai Cocktail

Makes 1 gallon mix

The mai tais made in the 1950s on Waikīkī Beach were both delicious and powerful. They were a far cry from the watered-down fruit-punchy versions you get in most lounges today. This is a recipe for a classic mai tai mix. You add rum according to your taste.

Mai Tai Mix:

1 cup 'ōkolehao whiskey (or your favorite bourbon)
1 bottle (fifth) orange curaçao
1/2 cup liliko'i juice
1 cup orange juice
1 cup pineapple juice
1 cup fresh lemon juice
1/2 cup orgeat syrup

Mix together to make 1 gallon. Keep in the refrigerator to make up mai tais.

To make an individual mai tai:
Fill your glass with crushed ice. Pour in 1 jigger of light Puerto Rican rum. Fill the glass with the Mai Tai Mix, leaving an inch at the top. Then float 1 jigger of heavy dark Jamaican rum on top. Garnish with mint, pineapple, and an orchid. Be as corny as you like.

COUNTRY CLUB ICED TEA

Makes 1 gallon

Almost every country club in Hawai'i and some restaurants make a version of this tea. The trick is to make it with plain ol' black tea and then add fruit juice and lots of fresh mint. Sometimes the juice is pineapple, sometimes it comes from an abundance of lemon trees in the backyard. One kama'āina family made a simple syrup by cooking the sugar first, thereby making it easier to dissolve. There is now a commercial version sold in cans. But fresh is still best.

1/2	gallon water
12	black tea bags
3	sprigs fresh mint
2	cups sugar
12	ounces pineapple juice
6	ounces lemon juice
	Pineapple spears and fresh mint sprigs, as garnish

In a large pot, bring the water to a boil. Steep the tea bags and fresh mint in the hot water. Remove the mint after 3 minutes, but continue to steep the tea until it is very dark. Remove the tea bags. Add the sugar and juices while the tea is still warm. Stir to dissolve the sugar. Pour into a gallon container (large mayonnaise jar) and add water to fill. Refrigerate. Serve with ice and garnishes.

KUKUIOLONO COCKTAIL

Makes 1 serving

There is a hill on the island of Kaua'i called "Kukuiolono," which means "the light of the god Lono." Sugar planter Walter McBride built his home atop this hill, and like many a neighbor island kama'āina became famous for his brand of country hospitality. He was especially well known for serving this cocktail to guests at his memorable lū'au. But be careful. Drink too many, and it will be more than the hill that gets lit. This recipe has been adapted from the Kāua'i Historical Society Cookbook.

1	part gin
2	parts fresh peach juice
	Sugar to taste
1 or 2	dashes of bitters
1	teaspoon orange juice

Mix all the ingredients together and shake well with ice. (Note: Canned peach or liliko'i juice can be used if fresh is not available.)

PĀHOEHOE COCKTAIL

Makes 1 serving

Every region has its own brand of homebrew whiskey. In Hawai'i it was 'ōkolehao, or more affectionately, "oke." Originally 'ōkolehao was distilled from the ti root (the ti plant is a staple in traditional Hawaiian cooking and was once found outside almost every kitchen), but later it became easier to produce from pineapple juice or rice. Kama'āina gentlemen from the middle of the last century and up through the 1950s kept their precious supply in large glass jugs and proudly pulled them out for good friends and family. This cocktail, which uses 'ōkolehao, was served at the graceful Mauna Kea Beach Hotel, built in the early 1960s on the Big Island of Hawai'i by hotelier and art collector Laurence Rockefeller. Pāhoehoe is the name for a type of smooth lava that flows from Hawai'i volcanoes. We're assuming the 'ōkolehao is equally smooth.

2 ounces 'ōkolehao (can substitute any bourbon-style whiskey)

2 ounces passion fruit juice

1 ounce grenadine

1 ounce lemon juice

Mix all ingredients in a blender with 3 to 4 cubes of ice. You may serve this plain in a glass or garnish with lemon peel and a sugar cube soaked in 151-proof rum.

POI COCKTAIL

Makes 1 drink

Kama'āina used to love this cocktail, but truthfully, it's rarely made anymore. It's both refreshing and comforting to the 'ōpu (stomach). Make it this way with the liquor or substitute 1/4 teaspoon vanilla extract for a virgin version.

1 cup whole milk

2 tablespoons mixed poi

3 teaspoons sugar

2 jiggers bourbon or brandy
   Crushed ice
   Dash of nutmeg

In a blender, place the milk, poi, sugar, bourbon or brandy (or $1/4$ teaspoon vanilla), and about 1 cup of crushed ice. Blend thoroughly and pour into a glass. Sprinkle the top with nutmeg.

Appetizers

BONELESS MOCHIKO CHICKEN BITS

Makes 20 pieces

My mother and her dear friend Elaine Shoda loved nothing better than packing lunches and kids on week-ends and heading for remote beaches. Here we swam in tidal pools while "Shoda" climbed over rocks and looked for limu (edible seaweed) and 'opihi (limpets), and my mother sought the shade of a kiawe tree. Shoda's lunches were always the best—cold bento food with fried chicken, salty-tasting rice balls filled with ume (red salted plums), and omelettes laced with shoyu and carrots. These mochiko chicken bits remind me of her picnics, although here they show up as appetizers. The use of Japanese mochiko (rice) flour, available in most Hawai'i markets and Asian markets on the mainland, is essential in this dish.

5	tablespoons cornstarch
4	tablespoons sugar
5	tablespoons shoyu
3	garlic cloves, crushed
2	eggs, beaten
$1/2$	cup chopped green onion, including green tops
$1/4$	cup sesame oil
3	tablespoons flour
6	tablespoons mochiko flour
	Salt to taste
1	tablespoon oyster sauce
5	pounds boneless chicken thighs
	Cooking oil such as peanut or canola

Mix all ingredients together except the chicken. Add chicken and marinate in a covered bowl or zippered plastic bag in the refrigerator for a minimum of 2 hours or overnight. Fry in hot oil 6 to 8 minutes or until browned and crisp. Drain on paper towels. Keep warm and serve with toothpicks. You may leave the bones in the chicken and make this an entrée or picnic dish.

CARAMELIZED MAUI ONION TART

Serves 6

Maui onions are so sweet that caramelizing gives them an almost jam-like quality. The ready-made puff pastry makes preparation easy. This tart can be served as an appetizer or a light lunch entrée.

4	slices bacon, chopped
3	tablespoons butter
4	pounds Maui onions, thinly sliced
	White pepper to taste
1	sheet ($1/_2$ 17.25-ounce box) frozen puff pastry, thawed

In a heavy skillet over medium heat, cook the bacon until golden, about 8 minutes. Reduce the heat to low and add the butter and onions. Sauté until the onions are brown and caramelized, about 1 hour. Season with white pepper. (At this point you can cover and chill the filling up to a day ahead.)

Roll out the pastry sheet to 13 inches square. Fit the pastry into an 11-inch tart pan with removable bottom. Trim the excess dough. Freeze the pastry for 30 minutes. Preheat the oven to 425 degrees F. Fill the crust with the onion mixture. Bake until the crust is golden, about 25 minutes. Cool slightly and serve.

EASY CHAR SIU BAO

Makes 12 small buns

Baked manapua is a popular lunch or snack, especially on Oʻahu, where there are many good Chinese bakeries. This is a quick adaptation for the home, made with handy commercially prepared dough.

Filling:

1	teaspoon sesame oil
3/4	pound char siu meat, minced
3	tablespoons chopped green onion
2 1/2	tablespoons sugar
4	teaspoons shoyu
	Salt to taste
2	teaspoons flour
2	teaspoons cornstarch
1/4	cup water
1	14-ounce package yeast bread mix, or 2 cans prepared dinner roll mix.

In a saucepan, over medium heat, heat the sesame oil and briefly sauté the char siu. Add the green onion, sugar, shoyu, and salt to the char siu. In a small bowl, combine the flour, cornstarch, and water. Stir mixture into the char siu mixture and continue to cook until thickened. Cool.

Preheat the oven to 400 degrees F. If using yeast bread mix, knead the dough for 1 or 2 minutes until smooth. Roll out dough flat and cut into 12 pieces. (If using canned rolls, open the package and roll out each individually.) Put a tablespoon of filling into the center of each piece of dough and wrap dough into a ball. Place seam side down on a greased baking sheet. If using the yeast bread mix, cover and allow to rise until doubled. The dinner roll mix can be baked immediately. Bake for 12 to 15 minutes, or until golden brown.

Hoku's 'Ahi Poke Dip

Makes about 4 cups

Hoku's in the Kahala Mandarin Oriental Hotel makes this spread to go with their freshly baked chiabatta bread. Try it with crackers for your next party.

2	cups mayonnaise
$1/2$	cup chopped pickled ginger (gari shoga)
$1/2$	cup chopped green onion, including some of the green tops
$1/2$	cup chopped Chinese parsley
$1/4$	cup toasted white sesame seeds
$1/2$	cup fresh lemon juice
$1/2$	cup shoyu
2	teaspoons freshly ground white pepper
$3/4$	cup diced fresh 'ahi

Place all the ingredients in a food processor or blender jar and process until smooth. Refrigerate until ready to use. If preparing ahead of time, mix the pepper and fresh 'ahi just before serving. Can be stored in the refrigerator up to a week before adding the pepper and 'ahi.

HOT CRAB DIP

Serves 6

There's nothing new about hot crab dip, yet we still love it. I almost like it better made with imitation crabmeat than with the real thing. Serve with crackers, or on top of Boboli pizza crusts, or as filling in tiny boiled red potatoes whose centers have been scooped out.

1	8-ounce package cream cheese, softened
1	cup crabmeat or imitation crabmeat
2	hard-boiled eggs, sieved
1	garlic clove, minced
1/2	cup mayonnaise
1	tablespoon chopped onion
1	teaspoon Colman's mustard
	Salt to taste

Preheat the oven to 325 degrees F. In a bowl, mix all the ingredients until combined. Pour into an ovenproof dish and bake for 20 minutes, or until hot and bubbly. Serve as you like.

HOT CURRIED NUTS

Makes 2$^1/_2$ cups

I first tried this with an abundance of macadamia nuts grown on the Carter estate, Kulamanu, on Maui, and given to my husband and me as a gift. They were so delicious, I now curry any kind of nuts I find on sale in the market.

1	tablespoon hot curry powder
1	tablespoon mild vegetable oil
11	ounces mixed nuts, such as cashews, macadamia, walnuts, almonds, pecans
1/2	teaspoon salt (delete if nuts are already salted)

In a heavy skillet over medium heat, cook the curry powder in the oil, stirring occasionally to release the flavors, about 5 minutes. Do not burn. Stir in the nuts and salt. Cook, stirring occasionally, until the nuts are toasted, about 5 minutes. Let cool to room temperature. The nuts will keep in an airtight container for up to 5 days.

MACADAMIA PESTO CHEESECAKE

Serves 16

When you need to serve a crowd, you want this appetizer cheesecake. Serve it with crackers during the holidays or any time of the year. If you don't have macadamia nuts, pine nuts (used in classic pesto) work just as well. If you don't have the fresh basil, substitute 1 cup parsley and 1 tablespoon dried basil.

1	cup dry breadcrumbs
1/4	cup butter, melted
1/4	cup olive oil
2	cups fresh basil leaves
	Salt to taste
1	clove garlic, halved
2	8-ounce packages cream cheese, softened
1	cup part-skim ricotta cheese
3	eggs
1/2	cup (2 ounces) grated Parmesan cheese
1/2	cup chopped macadamia nuts

Crust:

Preheat the oven to 350 degrees F. In a bowl, combine the breadcrumbs and melted butter. Press the mixture onto the bottom of a 9-inch springform pan. Bake for 10 minutes.

Filling:

Place the oil, basil, salt, and garlic in a blender. Cover and process on high until smooth. In a large bowl, combine the basil mixture with the cream cheese and ricotta cheese. Using an electric mixer at medium speed, blend until well mixed. Add the eggs 1 at a time and mix well. Blend in the Parmesan cheese and pour filling over the warm crust. Top with macadamia nuts. Bake at 325 degrees F. for 1 hour and 15 minutes, or until cheesecake is set and lightly browned. Loosen the cake from the rim of the pan; cool before removing the rim. Serve warm or at room temperature with your favorite assortment of crackers.

MANGO CHUTNEY AND AVOCADO SPREAD

Makes 5 cups

This is a nice twist on the standard guacamole and works as well with crackers as with chips. My hunch is that this spread originated when someone wanted to clean out all those partial jars of home-made mango chutney cluttering up the refrigerator.

4	ripe avocados, peeled, seeded, and chopped
1/4	cup mango chutney (commercial or homemade)
2	cloves garlic, peeled and halved
2	small limes, juiced
	Salt and pepper to taste
	Dash of Tabasco
1	cup tomato, seeded and chopped

Place 3 avocados, chutney, garlic, and lime juice in a blender and purée. Season with salt, pepper, and Tabasco. Add tomato and the remaining avocado and blend for only a few seconds. You want the guacamole to remain chunky. Chill and serve with crackers or chips.

GREEN OLIVE TAPENADE

Makes about 3/4 cup

1	large Maui onion, sliced into rings
8 to 10	cloves garlic
1	cup stuffed green olives, rinsed
2	teaspoons fresh thyme
2	teaspoons fresh marjoram
1/2	teaspoon red pepper flakes
	Dash of balsamic vinegar
1	teaspoon olive oil
	White pepper to taste

Grill the onion and garlic until lightly browned. Place in a food processor or blender with the olives, thyme, marjoram, and red pepper flakes. Chop until well blended. Add the vinegar, olive oil, and white pepper. Process another 10 seconds and place in a serving dish. Spread on bread toasted on the grill or crackers.

PAUWELA CAFE 'AHI POKI
Serves 12

This is Becky Speere's very healthy version.

2	pounds 'ahi, diced into $3/4$-inch pieces
$1^1/_2$	cups lemon juice
4	cucumbers, diced into $3/4$-inch pieces
6	tomatoes, diced into $3/4$-inch pieces
2	Maui onions, diced into $3/4$-inch pieces
$1/_2$	cup capers, drained
$1/_2$	cup extra virgin olive oil
4	teaspoons Hawaiian salt
$1/_2$	teaspoon black pepper
1	tablespoon dried oregano
1	teaspoon ground cumin
1	teaspoon Hawaiian chili paste*

In a small bowl, marinate the 'ahi in the lemon juice overnight in the refrigerator. Add the remaining ingredients and mix well. Serve with fresh mixed lettuces and taro chips.

* To make the Hawaiian chili paste: Mix 1 cup fresh Hawaiian chili peppers (puréed in a small food processor), 1/3 cup wine vinegar, 3 teaspoons chopped garlic, 1 teaspoon salt, and 1 tablespoon fish sauce (patis).

PIPIKAULA

Serves 12

The cowgirl-turned-folk-historian Inez Ashdown used to make a version of this traditional jerky with goat meat, as did many hunters on all islands. Instead of oven-drying, she would hang the marinated strips of meat in a homemade wood and screen box outdoors until it was "of good dryness." She would then throw it over hot coals to pūlehu, or cook until warm. It's particularly good with cold beer. This recipe was originally printed in an old benefit cookbook for Seabury Hall on Maui.

4	pounds flank steak or skirt steak, cut into strips 3 inches wide
1	cup shoyu
1	cup sugar
1	cup chopped green onion
$1/2$	cup vegetable oil
$1/2$	cup sesame oil
2	tablespoons toasted sesame seeds
2	Hawaiian chili peppers, seeded and chopped
$1/2$	cup honey

In a large bowl, combine the steak and all the ingredients except the honey. Marinate covered in the refrigerator for 48 hours, turning about 4 times. Preheat the oven to 250 degrees F. Place the steak on a rack with a drip pan and cook slowly for 4 to 5 hours, turning once. Baste with the honey about 10 minutes before removing. Cool and thinly slice before serving. Store in the refrigerator in an airtight container. To serve as a pupu, heat up a skillet and lightly pan fry.

POISSON CRU

Serves 10 to 12

This dish was introduced by Tahitians and can be made with any firm white-meat fish, although 'ahi and 'ono are favorites. It is prepared in much the same way the Mexicans prepare ceviche. The fish is "cooked" by the lime juice. You can buy frozen unsweetened coconut milk, or use the canned Asian variety. Some versions of this dish do not use coconut milk at all.

1	pound fresh 'ahi or 'ono
$1/2$	quart water with 2 tablespoons salt added
1	teaspoon salt
1	cup freshly squeezed lime juice
1	12-ounce can unsweetened coconut milk
1	medium tomato, coarsely chopped
$1/2$	medium onion, coarsely chopped
4	small red radishes, coarsely chopped
$1/2$	cup parsley, minced
	Salt and pepper to taste
4 to 5	drops Tabasco
	Lettuce leaves

Cut the fish into bite-sized pieces and soak in the salted water for 30 minutes. Drain well. Sprinkle fish with salt and lime juice and marinate in a nonreactive bowl for another 10 minutes, or until "cooked." Mix well and drain most of the liquid from fish. Add the coconut milk, tomato, onion, radish, parsley, salt, pepper, and Tabasco. Marinate for another 30 minutes. Serve with toothpicks as an appetizer or on lettuce as a first course.

Rumaki

Serves 4 to 6

There was a day when every silver tray at every cocktail party on Makiki Heights held piping hot rumaki. They may be old-fashioned, but they're still very good.

1   pound chicken livers
3   teaspoons shoyu
3   teaspoons brandy
2   5-ounce cans water chestnuts
1   pound bacon
     Toothpicks for skewers

In a bowl, marinate the chicken livers in the shoyu and brandy for 30 minutes. Cut the chicken livers, water chestnuts, and slices of bacon in half. Wrap the chicken liver and chestnut halves with the bacon and secure with a toothpick. Preheat the broiler. Place the rumaki on a baking sheet and broil for 4 to 5 minutes, or until the bacon is browned. Drain on paper towels and serve while still warm.

THE 'UKULELE: HAWAI'I'S "JUMPING FLEA"

When the sailing ship *Ravenscrag* from Madeira docked at Honolulu Harbor on August 23, 1879, there were 419 Portuguese settlers aboard. The story goes that after a grueling fifteen thousand miles over a period of four months, the immigrants were so happy to finally reach Hawai'i they broke into song, accompanied by their traditional instruments, to the delight of bystanders.

The Portuguese *braguinha*, as it was called in Madeira, or *cavaquinho* in Portugal, was the forerunner of the Hawaiian 'ukulele. The instrument was usually played along with the mandolin and guitar at country folk festivals like those following a grape harvest.

It's not known whether the 'ukulele (it literally means "jumping flea") got its name because the quick plucking of fingers across the instrument reminded Hawaiians of fleas, or because it was associated with an army officer named Edward Purvis. Purvis loved the 'ukulele and became quite a virtuoso in the late nineteenth century, playing for the royal court and amusing them with his fast movements and small stature. Hawaiians referred to him as "'Ukulele," and the instrument became "'Ukulele's instrument."

It is the simplicity and convenient size of the 'ukulele, as well as the ease of playing it, that have kept it the most well loved of Hawaiian instruments throughout the years. The 'ukulele is today the foremost symbol of Hawaiian music.

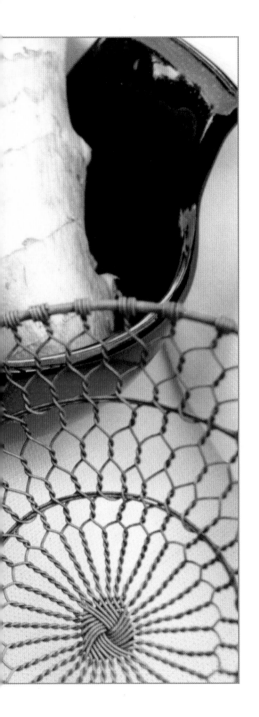

2

SOUPS AND SALADS

Nothing smells more like home to me than spicy bean soup simmering for hours on the back burner. Like wood smoke at twilight and the scent of freshly baked bread wafting out a kitchen window, it creates a wave of well-being no matter where I am. This is the smell that poured from the pineapple and sugar plantation camps of my youth, out the green-stained little houses all in a row—the homes of Portuguese Catholic families who arrived in the last century from Madeira and the Azores—and down the scrubbed white sidewalks to the boundary of a hibiscus hedge. This soup, introduced even in Hawai'i's tropical climate for the hearty nourishment it gave large, hard-working families, has been embraced by all ethnic groups and is now standard in country restaurants and bazaars.

Hawaiian soups and salads are a true blend of East and West, with the original recipes adapted to what was available here in the earlier part of this century. A good Japanese miso soup is as common in Hawai'i as a good chicken soup is in Manhattan. And it's often eaten as a cure for the same ailments.

27

I was first introduced to Chinese Chicken Salad back in the 1960s when Chinese friends were getting married and it was a popular buffet dish at weddings. The shredded lettuce, cilantro, sweet char siu pork, and tangy sesame dressing were a refreshing taste amidst all the traditional Cantonese dishes. Today there's a version of it on every restaurant menu.

Island salads can be as simple as marinated vegetables, used in the Japanese cucumber namasu (cucumbers and onion in rice vinegar) or lomi lomi salmon, the Hawaiian "salad" of fresh tomatoes, onion, and salt salmon in a cold brine.

Try any one of these and sense the trade winds.

$oups

CHILLED CUCUMBER-AVOCADO SOUP

Serves 6

When there are too many avocados on the ground, it's time to make this simple, refreshing cold soup.

1	large, ripe avocado, peeled and cut into 2-inch pieces
2	medium cucumbers, cut into 2-inch chunks
1	cup buttermilk
$1/2$	cup light cream
2	tablespoons chopped chives
1	garlic clove, minced
1	stalk green onion, chopped with green tops
	Salt and pepper to taste
$1/2$	teaspoon tarragon vinegar
$1/2$	cup sour cream or plain nonfat yogurt
2	cups chopped cucumber
1	avocado, peeled, seeded, and chopped
	Red tomato salsa, for garnish

In a blender or food processor, process the avocado and cucumbers with $1/2$ cup of the buttermilk until smooth. Add the remaining $1/2$ cup buttermilk, cream, chives, garlic, green onion, salt, and pepper. Finish by adding the tarragon vinegar and sour cream or nonfat yogurt. Process. Pour into a bowl and fold in the chopped cucumber and avocado. Chill for at least 2 hours to allow flavors to develop. Serve with salsa.

COCONUT-GINGER-CARROT SOUP
Serves 4

This truly tropical soup is so yummy you'll want to make another batch the next day. It's as exotic as the South Pacific and the South China Sea.

1	tablespoon canola oil
1	medium onion, chopped
2	pounds carrots, diced
4	quarter-sized pieces of fresh ginger, peeled and smashed
4	medium sweet potatoes, cut into large cubes
2^1/$_2$	cups or more chicken stock
	Salt and pepper to taste
	Dash of Tabasco
2 to 3	teaspoons fresh lemon juice
1	tablespoon honey
1	can coconut milk
	Chopped fresh cilantro for garnish

In a large saucepan, heat the oil. Add the onion and cook over medium heat for about 5 minutes. Add the carrots and ginger and cook another 5 minutes. Add the sweet potatoes, chicken stock, salt, and pepper. Let the soup come to a boil. Simmer until the carrots and potatoes are tender, about 25 minutes. Cool slightly. Place the carrot and sweet potato mixture, retaining 1 cup of the liquid from the soup, into a blender or food processor and process until smooth. Add Tabasco, lemon juice, honey, and the retained 1 cup of liquid and purée until smooth. Return mixture to the saucepan and reheat on low. Add the coconut milk and stir to mix thoroughly. If the soup is too thick, thin with more chicken stock.

FISHCAKE MISO SOUP

Serves 6

If you live on the mainland, an Asian market is the best source for the ingredients in this soup. The flavor is clean and slightly fishy.

1/4	cup white miso
2	tablespoons water
1/2	pound raw Chinese fishcake
2	tablespoons finely diced carrots
1	tablespoon minced green onion
5	cups water
1	tablespoon sake
2	tablespoons hondashi
1/2	cup tofu, cubed
	Green onion and wakame (seaweed that has been reconstituted in warm water) for garnish

In a small bowl, mix the miso with 2 table-spoons water and set aside. In another small bowl, mix the fishcake, carrots, and green onion together. Bring about 5 cups water to a boil in a large pot. Using a teaspoon, drop the fishcake mixture like dumplings into the hot water. Add the miso mixture, sake, hondashi, and tofu. Simmer for about 7 minutes, or until done. Garnish with green onion and wakame and serve.

SHEP GORDON'S MAUI ONION AND GINGER SOUP

Serves 4

Shep Gordon is a Hollywood-producer-turned-avid-gourmet. He now makes Hawai'i his home. His friends and houseguests love this soup. You will too.

4	large Maui onions, sliced
2	tablespoons butter
3	tablespoons freshly grated ginger
4	sprigs fresh thyme, or 1 teaspoon dried
1	cup dry white wine
1	quart chicken broth
1/2	pint half and half

In a saucepan, sauté the onions in the butter over medium heat. Add the ginger and continue to cook until the onions are clear, but not browned. Add the thyme, wine, and chicken broth and bring to a boil. Continue to cook for 30 minutes. Remove from heat and cool. Purée the soup in a blender or food processor. Add the half and half and return to the heat. This soup can be served hot or cold with a dollop of sour cream.

PAPAYA-COCONUT BISQUE

Serves 4

This bisque is so rich and creamy it could almost be dessert. This is not for anyone on a strict diet, but it's wonderful for a festive holiday meal. If you cannot find coconut liqueur, the non-alcoholic cream-of-coconut mix used for piña coladas, found in the liquor department, will work. This is the ultimate tropical soup.

8	ripe papayas
4	ounces bottled mineral water
1	pint heavy cream
$1/2$	cup coconut liqueur or Coco Lopez mix
2	cups half and half
4	sprigs mint for garnish

Slice 4 of the papayas in half, seed, and scoop out some of the meat (leaving about a $1/4$-inch border of meat intact). Use these halves as containers for the soup. Seed and scoop the meat out of the other 4 papayas and discard the shells. Place the papaya meat in a blender or food processor. Add the mineral water (use 7-Up or Sprite if you are serving this as a dessert), heavy cream, coconut liqueur, and half and half. Process until smooth. If this is too much for your blender, process the liquid and cream first separately, then the papaya with a small amount of liquid. Pour into a bowl, cover, and refrigerate. To serve, pour into the reserved papaya boats and garnish with a sprig of mint. (Note: If you double this recipe, cut back the liqueur to $3/4$ cup for 8).

PORTUGUESE BEAN SOUP
Serves 10

This version of the classic soup is old-style, which means beginning from scratch and using spices such as cinnamon and cloves. Kale was sometimes used instead of head cabbage. If there was a spare sweet potato in the larder, it went into the soup too. The roast beef bones and roasting process in this recipe are responsible for much of its goodness. However, you can substitute ham hocks and skip the roasting and still be pleased with the results.

3	pounds beef bones (or 4 ham hocks)
2 to 3	pounds lean, cubed stew beef
4	cloves garlic, sliced
4	stalks celery, chopped, including leaves
1	onion, cubed
2	bay leaves
4	sprigs parsley, chopped
2	15-ounce cans kidney beans
1	28-ounce can whole tomatoes
2	carrots, peeled and cubed
2	onions, cubed

$1/2$	head cabbage, sliced
6	potatoes, peeled and cubed
1	cup chopped kale or watercress, optional
2	Portuguese linguisa sausages (about 8 ounces each), sliced in chunks
1	teaspoon Portuguese spice (or $1/2$ teaspoon each anise, cinnamon, cloves, and pepper)
	Salt to taste

Preheat the oven to 400 degrees F. Place the beef bones and stew meat in a roasting pan and roast for 30 minutes, until browned. Cool and cut the stew meat into small cubes. In a large stock pot, over medium-high heat, place the oven-browned bones and meat and cover with water. Add garlic, celery, onion, bay leaves, and parsley and simmer at least 4 hours to make stock. Strain and discard solid ingredients. Skim any fat that rises to the top. Add the kidney beans, tomatoes, carrots, onions, cabbage, potatoes, kale or watercress, sausage, and spices to the stock and cook for at least $1^1/2$ hours longer. Serve with Portuguese sweet bread or a crusty, peasant-style bread and butter.

TARO LEAF AND CHICKEN SOUP

Serves 4

Taro leaf, or lū'au, is a delicious but underused green available fresh or frozen in most local markets. It's often compared to spinach, which you can substitute when lū'au is unavailable. If you've never cooked it before, don't let it intimidate you. Along with the taro corm (kalo) and the stalks (hāhā), lū'au is one of the staples of the native Hawaiian diet. It is high in nutrients such as vitamins A and C, folic acid, magnesium, calcium, and iron.

2	tablespoons oil
1	Maui onion, sliced
2	cloves garlic, minced
5	slices fresh ginger
2	quarts chicken stock
12	taro leaves, cleaned and deveined (see below), or 1 package frozen taro leaves
1	pound chicken breasts or thighs, cut in strips
1	tablespoon Hawaiian salt
	White pepper to taste

In a large soup pot over medium-high heat, sauté the onion, garlic, and ginger in the oil until golden brown. Add the chicken stock and bring to a boil. Reduce the heat and add the chopped taro (lū'au) leaves to the stock. Simmer for 35 minutes. Add the chicken, salt, and pepper. Cook for another 10 minutes.

To prepare fresh lū'au: Wash the lū'au leaves well under running water, or in a sink filled with water. Some people put a handful of Hawaiian salt into the water to loosen any bugs that may be clinging to the leaves. Trim the stalks. Chop the taro leaves.

SALADS

CHINESE CHICKEN SALAD

Serves 2

I especially like the sweetness of this salad dressing. If you don't have, or don't like, any of the ingredients in the salad, change them. Cashews or peanuts will work just as well as slivered almonds. Wonton pi chips or canned chow mein noodles can be substituted for the wonton sticks. Mesclun gourmet salad mix works as well as iceberg and romaine. For me, though, the cilantro, or Chinese parsley, is an essential flavor.

6 to 8	cups shredded iceberg and romaine lettuce
1/4	cup finely chopped green onion
1/4	cup finely chopped fresh cilantro (Chinese parsley)
3	large cooked chicken breasts, boneless and skinless
1/2	cup char siu pork, slivered
4	carrots, shredded
1	cup crispy wonton sticks
2	tablespoons sesame seeds, toasted
1/4	cup slivered almonds, toasted (optional)

Dressing:

3	tablespoons hoisin sauce
1/2	cup plum sauce
2	tablespoons shoyu
2	tablespoons sesame oil
1/4	cup red wine vinegar
2	teaspoons lemon juice
1	teaspoon ground ginger
1/2	teaspoon dry mustard
	Dash of cayenne pepper
	Pinch of sugar
1/4	cup vegetable oil

Chop all the vegetables for the salad. In a large salad bowl, toss together all the ingredients. Add salad dressing to taste and serve.

To make the dressing: Whisk all the ingredients together and store in the refrigerator until ready to use. Keeps about 2 weeks.

FRESH OGO SALAD

Serves 4

This delicious ocean salad may be an acquired taste. Look for the different kinds of ogo, or seaweed, in the fish market section of island markets.

1   cup fresh red ogo

1   cup fresh green ogo

1   cup brown ogo

Dressing:

$^1/_4$ cup shoyu

$^1/_8$ cup rice wine vinegar

$^1/_2$ teaspoon sesame oil

$^1/_4$ teaspoon black pepper

1   large tomato, diced

$^1/_2$ finely chopped Maui onion

2   green onions, chopped, with the green tops

1   teaspoon grated fresh ginger

Bring a pot of water to a boil and blanch the ogo quickly. Remove and plunge into a bowl filled with ice water to cool. Squeeze out the excess water and pat dry. Put the ogo in a salad bowl and toss with the dressing. Chill before serving.

To make the dressing: Combine all the dressing ingredients and whisk together.

KEOKI'S PEA SALAD

Serves 6

My husband talks lovingly about the salad of petite peas made for his friend, the late George Carter, when they spent weekends many years ago at a shared cabin at Pālehua on O'ahu. George never actually made the salad himself. It was prepared by his cook, along with the fresh-squeezed orange juice he liked the moment he awoke—which was usually quite late in the day.

1	10-ounce package frozen petite peas, thawed
1	cup chopped celery
1/4	cup chopped green onion, with the green tops
1	cup cashews or chopped macadamia nuts
1/4	cup bacon, cooked crisp, drained, and crumbled
1	cup sour cream
1/4	cup bottled Italian or French dressing
	Salt and pepper to taste

In a bowl, combine the peas, celery, green onion, nuts, and bacon. Mix together the sour cream and bottled dressing. Toss the vegetables with the dressing and season with salt and pepper. One cup of water chestnuts can be substituted for the nuts if you prefer. Can be made ahead and served chilled.

OLD-FASHIONED FRENCH DRESSING

Makes 2 1/2 cups

My father, Pete St. Sure, made the thickest, richest French dressing when he and my stepmother, Lita, ran Buzz's Wharf at Mā'alaea in the 1970s. I'd always heard he made the dressing with tomato soup, so I was delighted to find this recipe in an old community cookbook.

1	can condensed tomato soup
2	tablespoons Maui onion, chopped
2	teaspoons mustard
3/4	cup brown sugar
1/2	cup canola oil
2/3	cup red wine vinegar
1	clove garlic, peeled and halved
1/2	teaspoon Colman's dry mustard
2	tablespoons Worcestershire sauce
	Salt and pepper to taste

Place all the ingredients in a blender and process until smooth. Keep in a jar and refrigerate until ready to use. Keeps about 2 weeks.

Tofu Salad

Serves 6 to 8

This layered salad is simple to make and always tastes fresh and clean. It's ideal to take to the office for lunch or on a picnic.

1   block firm tofu, cut in $1/2$-inch cubes

$1/3$ cup canola oil

1   clove garlic, halved

1   medium Maui onion, sliced

2   medium ripe tomatoes, chopped

1   small can water-packed tuna, drained

$1/2$ cup green onion, chopped, with some green tops

2   sprigs cilantro, chopped

$1/2$ cup shoyu

    A few drops of sesame oil

    A few drops of garlic oil

In the bottom of a flat pan or plastic container, layer the tofu. In a small saucepan, heat the oil and garlic and cook until the garlic is browned, but not burned. Set aside to cool. Layer the onion on top of the tofu. Layer the tomatoes on top of the onion. Next, layer the crumbled tuna. On top of that, layer the green onion and cilantro. Put the shoyu, sesame oil, and garlic oil into a glass jar and shake well. Just before serving, pour the dressing over the layered salad. Keep refrigerated until ready to eat.

WON BOK SALAD

Serves 6

Won bok is otherwise known as napa cabbage. A friend describes this salad as being "more than the sum of its parts." It's sort of "goopy" looking, but very delicious. Every time I make it, I'm asked for the recipe.

1	can chow mein noodles
1/2	cup slivered almonds
2	tablespoons sesame seeds
3/4	cup (or more) mayonnaise
4	tablespoons shoyu
1	teaspoon sesame oil
1	won bok cabbage, finely shredded
1/2	pound fresh mushrooms, sliced
1	can sliced water chestnuts
2	tablespoons cilantro (Chinese parsley), chopped
4	green onions, chopped, with some green tops

Preheat the oven to 350 degrees F. On a cookie sheet, toast the noodles, almonds, and sesame seeds for 5 minutes. Do not burn. Remove and cool. Mix the mayonnaise, shoyu, and sesame oil to make a dressing. Thin dressing with a small amount of water if you prefer it thinner. Toss the won bok, mushrooms, water chestnuts, cilantro, and onion in a salad bowl. Mix in the noodles, almonds, sesame seeds, and dressing. Serve immediately.

HAWAIIAN QUILTS: CRAFT AND CULTURE COMBINE

Missionaries outfitting themselves for the Sandwich Islands in 1834 were instructed to bring items for the cooler months. These included two pairs of woolen pantaloons, one cloak, four pairs of gloves, and three bed quilts.

It was the bed quilts that impressed Hawaiians the most. Until that time they bedded down on mattresses made of many layers of lauhala (pandanus) mats covered with a kapa moe, a sleeping cloth made up of four or five thin sheets of kapa (pounded from mulberry bark and imprinted with designs).

The quilts, many of them New England–style patchwork, were fascinating and useful. Soon cotton fabric, thread, and needles became especially prized throughout the Hawaiian community.

It is not certain exactly when Hawaiian quilting took on its unique appearance, but by 1874, Emma Lyman of Hilo had four Hawaiian-style quilts in her possession when she arrived on Kaua'i to marry young Samuel Whitney Wilcox, the son of another missionary family.

Hawaiian quilts, unlike those of most of their American cousins, were made of a single piece of fabric appliquéd with white thread upon a white background. An "echo" stitch was then used to outline the design, giving the appearance of ripples on the quilt.

Quilters personalized the quilts to such a degree that the designs reflected deeply held beliefs and lore within the Hawaiian culture. They took motifs either from the lush nature that surrounded them or from special events in their lives.

Quilt designs were associated with their creators, and patterns were fiercely guarded. Each quilter named her design in the poetic and floral style of the time, using Hawaiian expressions to explain the inspiration for the design.

Popular designs included the "'ulu" (breadfruit), "kukui" (candlenut tree), and "loke-lani" (pink cottage rose). More complex designs had such names as "Ka Ipu Kukui O Kahului" (Chandelier of Kahului).

When the Hawaiian kingdom was overthrown by American businessmen, many of them missionary descendants, in 1893, and displaying the Hawaiian flag became an act of treason, quilters revolted in a quiet way by designing a quilt with several variations called "Ka'u Hae Aloha," or "My Beloved Flag." In that way, they felt they could still sleep each night under the flag of Hawai'i.

A Hawaiian quilt is always given in love with much of the spirit of the maker still attached. In the very earliest days of quilting, Hawaiian women often destroyed their patterns and had their quilts buried with them because they felt they contained their mana, or spirit.

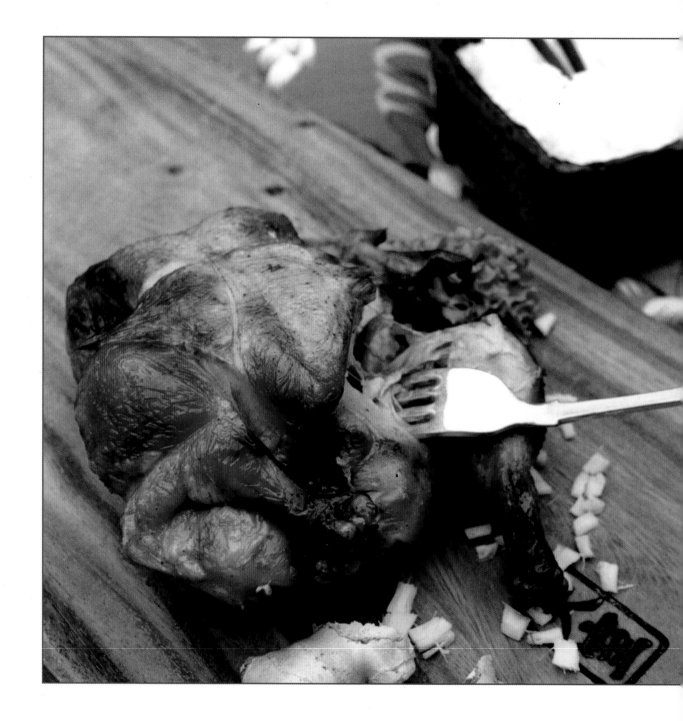

3

CHICKEN, PORK, BEEF AND LAMB

As a kid, I'd beg each weekend to stay at my grand-mother's house and sleep on her big pūne'e with her and at least two other cousins. Among the dishes we loved was something she called simply "boiled hamburger." I admit that doesn't exactly sound like culinary heaven, but we loved it, and it went very nicely over hot rice.

When I asked her what made it taste so good, she said it was just ketchup, Worcestershire sauce, and shoyu—the three magic ingredients of "local-style" stews and gravy. You will find that combination again and again in island cooking.

It's not uncommon in Hawai'i for a Japanese country stir-fry dish such as Chicken Hekka (chicken pieces with tofu, green onion, bean sprouts, and vegetables in a sweet and salty soy sauce) to be the main dish at a Portuguese family table.

There is so much intermarriage between the ethnic groups that foods are no longer enjoyed just in the homes they started out in. Children named Smith could as likely have a lunch of noodles at their Chinese grandmother's house as tuna sandwiches at home. Any island potluck dinner will likely include everything from sushi to potato salad and hamburgers on the grill.

The recipes in this chapter run the gamut from the traditional laulau to pūlehu, or barbecued short ribs. The Portuguese pork roast makes a perfect company or holiday dish, as does the Chicken Laulau with Curry Sauce (page 107).

43

CHICKEN

CHICKEN TINOLA
Serves 4

Chicken Tinola is a warm and comforting dish from the Philippines. Pipinola squash is also called chayote squash, and can be used if you can't find green papaya. The marungay leaves are often hard to come by. You may have to visit Chinatown or a Filipino market.

2	garlic cloves, sliced
3	pieces fresh ginger, sliced and smashed
1	Maui onion, sliced
2	tablespoons oil
1	whole chicken, $3^1/_2$ to 4 pounds, cut up, with skin and bones removed
1 to 2	cups water or chicken broth
2	cups green papaya or pipinola squash, peeled, seeded, and cut into 1-inch chunks
1	cup marungay leaves (optional)
2	tablespoons patis fish sauce or salt and pepper to taste

In a deep skillet over medium-high heat, sauté the garlic, ginger, and onion in the oil until lightly browned. Add the chicken and sauté for 2 to 3 minutes, until lightly browned. Add the water or chicken broth, bring to a boil, and simmer about 15 minutes. Add the papaya or pipinola and marungay leaves (if using) and continue cooking until just tender, about 5 minutes. Season to taste with fish sauce.

CHICKEN HEKKA

Serves 6

This dish was once Japanese sukiyaki. Over the years, plantation cooks changed and adapted it, using available ingredients. Today variations of "hekka" can be found at plate lunch counters, hotel buffets, and home parties. Bruno Wong, a pressman at the old Maui News, used to cook up a batch in the back lot on Friday at pau hana (finish work) time. Reporters, ad salesmen, layout staff, and circulation people would gather to drink beer and wind down from the week. Bruno would whip up his hekka in a large wok over kiawe (mesquite) charcoal set in half a metal drum. When it was done, we'd sit around on the asphalt on folding metal chairs, talking, laughing, and devouring the hekka on paper plates with cheap wooden chopsticks. It's a scene repeated at many job sites all over Hawai'i.

1	3.5-ounce bundle dried (cellophane) long rice noodles
5	dried shiitake mushrooms
1	pound boneless chicken thighs
1	tablespoon shoyu
4	tablespoons sake (Japanese rice wine) or whiskey
1	tablespoon peanut or canola oil
1/2	cup brown or raw sugar
1	large onion, sliced
1/2	cup shoyu
1	8-oz. can button mushrooms
1	8-oz. can sliced bamboo shoots
1	package aburage (fried tofu)
1	block Japanese tofu, cubed
4	stalks green onion, sliced diagonally into 2-inch pieces

Soak the rice noodles and mushrooms separately in warm water for about 1 hour to hydrate. Cut the chicken into 1-inch pieces and marinate with 1 tablespoon shoyu and 1 tablespoon of the sake. Drain shiitake mushrooms and cut off stems. Slice mushrooms. Heat oil in a wok on fairly high heat. Stir-fry chicken to sear for 2 to 3 minutes. Add sugar and onion and stir-fry another 2 minutes. Add 1/2 cup shoyu and remaining 3 tablespoons sake. Stir. Add button mushrooms, bamboo shoots, and drained long rice. Stir again until heated. Next add aburage, tofu, and green onion just to heat through. If there is not enough liquid, add water or chicken broth. Serve with hot rice.

'ONO SWEET-SOUR CHICKEN SPARERIBS

Serves 4 to 6

In this dish, the meat is just a medium for the flavor of the sauce—which is classic plantation Hawai'i. This recipe was probably once Chinese, but over the years changed to become simply "local." It's still a favorite at potluck gatherings and becomes a quick weekday dinner when served with steamed rice. If you substitute chicken drumettes, you can serve 18 appetizers.

2	tablespoons vegetable oil
2	pounds chicken thighs
$1/2$	cup water
$1/3$	cup shoyu
$1/3$	cup firmly packed brown sugar
$1/4$	cup apple or orange juice
2	tablespoons ketchup
1	tablespoon cider or rice wine vinegar
1	clove garlic, pressed
1	green onion, thinly sliced, with the green top
$1/2$	teaspoon crushed red pepper
1	tablespoon freshly grated ginger root
1	tablespoon cornstarch
1	tablespoon water
1	tablespoon black bean sauce (dau see), optional
	Green onion, sliced diagonally for garnish
	Sesame seeds, toasted, for garnish

Add oil to a large frying pan with nonstick finish. Heat pan over medium-high heat until a few drops of water sprinkled on the surface sizzle. Add chicken pieces and sauté about 5 to 7 minutes, turning frequently until lightly browned on all sides. Combine next 10 ingredients and add to chicken. Bring to a boil, cover, and reduce heat to simmer for 20 minutes. In a small bowl, mix together cornstarch and water. Add to chicken and cook, stirring until sauce thickens and glazes. If you like black bean flavor, you can add a tablespoon of black bean sauce at this point. Garnish with green onion slices and sesame seeds.

PETE'S ROASTED TERIYAKI CHICKEN

Serves 4

Teriyaki is a classic island sauce used on everything from beef and chicken to fish. This is my father's recipe, unique in that the sauce is cooked before being used as a marinade or basting sauce.

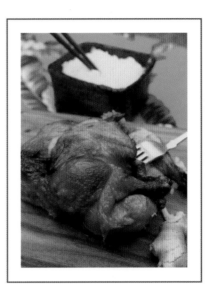

1	cup shoyu
1	cup sugar
1	3-inch piece ginger, peeled and sliced
4	cloves garlic, peeled and crushed
2	tablespoons bourbon
1	3$^1/_2$-pound chicken

Cook the shoyu and sugar in a small saucepan over medium-low heat until the sugar dissolves, about 2 minutes. Stir in the ginger, garlic, and bourbon and cook 30 minutes. Remove the ginger and garlic. Pour $^1/_4$ cup of the sauce into a small mixing bowl and store the additional for later use. It will keep in the refrigerator for up to 1 week. Makes 2 cups sauce.

Preheat the oven to 375 degrees F. Rinse the chicken and pat dry. Tie the legs together with kitchen string. Using a brush, coat the chicken with sauce inside the cavity and out. Place the chicken in a baking pan and roast for 1 hour, basting every 15 minutes. If you want a darker bird, baste more often. The chicken is done when you pierce the leg with a knife and the juice runs clear. Take the chicken out and allow it to rest for 15 minutes before carving.

PORK

PINACBET

Serves 6

Pinacbet is an Ilocano (Filipino) dish that always includes eggplant and bittermelon (pareia). The best eggplant for most Asian dishes is the small, thin variety often called Japanese eggplant. Avoid the large, globe egg-plants used in many Italian dishes, as they become too pulpy and soak up too much oil. You can use any cooked meat in place of the pork. This dish tastes best eaten the day it's made, since reheating may make the flavors too strong.

3   Japanese eggplants, cut into 2-inch chunks
2   medium bittermelons; scoop out center and cut into 2-inch chunks
1   tomato, cut into chunks
     Optional: 2 cups long beans, cut into 2-inch pieces,
     bagoong (fish sauce) to taste
3   cloves minced garlic
2   tablespoons oil
1   pound pork, in small, thin slices
1   Maui onion, cut into chunks
1   piece fresh ginger
3   tablespoons patis fish sauce (or more to taste)
1/2 cup water
     Salt and pepper to taste

Wash and cut the vegetables. Set aside. In a hot skillet or wok, sauté the garlic in oil, being careful not to burn it. Add the pork and sauté until lightly browned. Add the onion, then the ginger, fish sauce, and water. When the water boils, add first the eggplant, then the bittermelon when the egg-plant is half-cooked. Add the tomato last. Cover, reduce heat, and steam for about 15 minutes. Stir carefully, or the bittermelon will become more bitter tasting. Serve with rice.

PORK AND CLAMS

(Cataplana)

Serves 4

The Portuguese who immigrated to the islands brought with them hearty "stick to your ribs" cuisine. This dish of pork and clams is a marvelous example.

2	pounds boneless pork butt, cut into 1-inch cubes
1$^1/_2$	cups white wine
2	cloves garlic, peeled and chopped
1	teaspoon liquid smoke
	Salt and pepper to taste
2	bay leaves
$^1/_4$	cup or less olive oil
4	teaspoons paprika
2	medium onions, peeled and thinly sliced
2	pounds small clams in the shell

Place the pork in a large bowl. Mix together the wine, garlic, liquid smoke, salt, pepper, and bay leaves. Pour the mixture over the meat and marinate for 2 hours. Drain the meat and reserve the marinade.

Heat 2 tablespoons or less of the olive oil in a heavy frying pan. Brown the pork cubes. Place the meat in an 8-quart stovetop casserole and add the marinade and paprika. Simmer the meat uncovered in the juices until they almost evaporate, about 45 minutes. Skim the fat and discard the bay leaves. In another saucepan, sauté the onions in the remaining olive oil until tender. Add the clams, salt, and pepper. Cook over high heat, covered, for 5 minutes, or until clams open. Add the clams and juice to the pork and heat through. Serve with hot rice or boiled potatoes.

TRADITIONAL LAULAU

Makes 4

In our family, making laulau every New Year's Day was a tradition. The real work was left to my father, who made it his own personal project. We all gathered midday in the front yard and under the carport hung with blue plastic tarp to ward off the occasional winter drizzle. Relatives we rarely saw dropped by to "talk story" and watch football on the tiny portable set my father set up on a picnic table. Garage and carport parties are typical among Hawai'i's working people.

24	lū'au leaves (taro—or substitute fresh spinach)
1	pound salted butterfish or salmon (or substitute salted cod)
1¹/₂	tablespoons Hawaiian rock salt (kosher)
2	pounds pork shoulder, cut in 1- to 2-inch cubes
8	ti leaves (or substitute corn husks or parchment paper) String to tie
4	cooking bananas, left in skins
4	sweet potatoes or yams, left in skins

Wash the taro leaves thoroughly and remove stems and fibrous part of the vein. If the fish is very salty, cover it with water in a bowl, soak for 1 to 2 hours, and drain. Rub the salt into the pork and set aside.

Arrange 5 or 6 taro leaves in the palm of your hand and place a piece of pork and a piece of fish in the middle. Fold the leaves over the pork and fish to form a bundle.

Prepare the ti leaves by cutting the stiff center rib and stripping it off to make the leaf pliable. Place the taro leaf bundle at one end of the leaf and roll it up. Place another ti leaf across the bundle in the other direction and roll. Tie the ti leaf bundle securely with household string and knot.

Place the raw laulau bundle in a steamer with water in the bottom. Steam the laulau for 4 to 6 hours, checking the water and adding to it as necessary. The time will vary according to the density of the laulau. Add the bananas and sweet potatoes to the steamer during the last hour.

Vinha d'Ahlos

Serves 6

The Portuguese are responsible for this highly aromatic dish made often during holidays or for Sunday dinner. Garlic and vinegar are the elements that fill the house with a sense of comfort and joy.

1	3- to 4-pound boneless pork butt or shoulder roast
2 to 4	cloves garlic
1 to 3	small red Hawaiian chili peppers
1	bottle white wine
$^1/_4$	cup white or cider vinegar
2 to 3	bay leaves
1	teaspoon paprika
	Salt and pepper to taste
	Flat leaf parsley for garnish

Carve the pork roast into 1-inch chunks. Mince the garlic and cut the chili peppers in half. In a large nonreactive bowl, mix the garlic, chili peppers, wine, vinegar, bay leaves, paprika, salt, and pepper. Marinate the meat in the mixture overnight in a covered container in the refrigerator. (Can be marinated up to 2 days.)

Preheat the oven to 450 degrees F. Remove the chilies and pour off the marinade. Place the meat in a roasting pan and turn the heat down to 325 degrees. Cook the meat until done, about 2 hours. Peeled and quartered potatoes can be added to the pan during the last hour. Pour a little water or reserved marinade in the bottom of the pan if it is too dry or starting to burn. This dish can be made on top of the stove by adding a little olive oil to a dutch oven and browning the meat on all sides. Add a little water to the pan, cover, and simmer for 1 hour and 45 minutes, or until done.

B<small>EEF</small>

HAWAIIAN SHORT RIBS

Serves 4 to 6

Very hearty, this dish can easily be made ahead for a crowd. Be sure to skim off as much fat as possible and add a little water to thin the sauce if necessary.

- $1/2$ cup flour
- 3   pounds beef short ribs, trimmed of fat and cut into 2-inch pieces
- 2   large onions, sliced
- 1   cup ketchup
- 2   tablespoons shoyu
- 2   tablespoons Worcestershire sauce
- 3   tablespoons cider vinegar
- $1/2$ cup sugar
- 1   cup water
- 1   8-ounce can sliced water chestnuts, drained
- Chopped parsley for garnish

Preheat the oven to 325 degrees F. Put the flour and short ribs into a zippered plastic or brown paper bag and shake to coat. Put the generously floured ribs in a deep casserole dish and cover with the sliced onions. In a bowl, combine the ketchup, shoyu, Worcestershire sauce, vinegar, sugar, and water. Mix well and pour over the ribs and onions. Cover and bake for 3 hours. Skim off fat before adding the water chestnuts. If you make this a day ahead, put it in the refrigerator and skim off the fat that rises to the top. Serve with hot rice and garnish with the chopped parsley.

PŪLEHU SHORT RIBS

Serves 6

Pūlehu in Hawaiian means "to grill, or barbecue." This version is uniquely island in flavor and standard fare at weekend beach picnics or country cookouts. The preparation is simple, but the minute the ribs hit the hot grill everyone will begin to gather for a taste. Don't be polite. Just pick one up with your fingers and chew. Make sure you have plenty of napkins.

3	pounds beef short ribs
$^{1}/_{2}$	cup shoyu
$^{1}/_{2}$	cup ketchup
$^{3}/_{4}$	cup brown sugar
3	teaspoons sherry
3	teaspoons Hawaiian salt (or kosher salt)
4	pieces fresh gingerroot the size of a quarter, peeled and mashed
2 to 3	cloves garlic, sliced and mashed

Place the short ribs in a pan or zippered plastic bag. Mix all the remaining ingredients and pour over the ribs. Marinate for one day, turning occasionally. Barbecue ribs over a charcoal fire—kiawe (mesquite), if it's available—and baste once or twice during cooking. This is a tough cut of meat, but the marinating helps soften the texture. Allow approximately 15 to 20 minutes on each side, then check for doneness. The time will vary with the thickness of the meat.

Lamb

Ni‘ihau Lamb Shanks
Serves 6

These hearty lamb shanks are braised in a tart, sweet sauce typical of island cooking. Chinese soy sauce, or Japanese "shoyu," combined with ketchup, brown sugar, and vinegar, are flavorings used in many stews or meat dishes.

$2/3$	cup ketchup
$1/2$	cup vinegar
$1/2$	cup water
$1/4$	cup shoyu
1	8-ounce can crushed pineapple, drained
$1/4$	cup brown sugar
1	teaspoon salt
$1/2$	teaspoon nutmeg
2	teaspoons grated fresh ginger
1	onion, thinly sliced
6	lamb shanks

Preheat the oven to 350 degrees F. In a saucepan, mix together everything except the lamb shanks. Simmer, uncovered, over low heat for about 30 minutes. Place lamb shanks in an ovenproof dish and pour hot sauce over them. Cover and bake for $2^1/2$ to 3 hours, or until lamb is tender. If the sauce in the pan evaporates, add water and continue to cook. Place the cooked lamb on a serving platter and keep warm.

To make gravy:
Strain and skim the fat off the pan juices. Bring juices to a boil and thicken with $2^1/2$ tablespoons cornstarch mixed with an equal amount of water. Stir constantly until you get a thickened gravy. Spoon pan gravy over lamb shanks and serve. Remaining gravy may be passed at the table.

NĀ PANIOLO: HAWAI'I'S ROMANTIC COWBOYS

The paniolo, or Hawaiian cowboy, tradition in Hawai'i dates back to the 1830s—even before the heyday of the American west. In 1832, Don Luzada and two other vaqueros arrived on the Big Island of Hawai'i to teach Native Hawaiians how to manage the wild cattle roaming their forests. At the request of Kamehameha III, the Mexican vacqueros (California was then part of Mexico) brought with them their Spanish-rigged saddles, braided skin ropes, and guitars, creating for Hawai'i a distinctively different kind of cowhand.

Longhorned cattle (called pua'a pipi because they looked like large pigs) were first brought to Hawai'i in 1793 by Captain George Vancouver as a gift to Kamehameha I. However, by the time they arrived, most of the cattle had either died or were in extremely poor condition.

Because of their condition, Kamehameha I placed a 10-year kapu, or ban, on killing them. Unfortunately, that was just enough time for them to breed excessively and begin to run wild in island forests. Within a very short time they were a dangerous nuisance to the Hawaiians, who were forced to protect their taro, bananas, and houses by building rock walls to keep them out. Prior to the introduction of the vacquero, unsavory bullock hunters had been employed to go into the forests and destroy the wild cattle. The hunters, often drunkards and murderers off ships, had been considered the "dregs of society." The coming of the vacquero meant the end of this practice.

Horses had already been introduced to Hawai'i from California by Captain Richard Cleveland in 1803. Like the cattle, they too were allowed to roam free and adapt to their new environment.

By this time, the sandalwood trade of the early 1800s was winding down, and Hawaiian forests were sadly depleted. Many of the Hawaiian chiefs were looking for other products to sell to the ships putting in at island harbors. Salt, fresh meat, and hides for leather seemed like a good replacement.

Paniolo (old-timers often prefer "paniola") is the Hawaiian translation for the word Español. Most of the first paniolo were Hawaiian, although over the years every introduced ethnic group produced cowboys. They adopted the vaquero dress—a wide-brimmed black hat turned up in front, baggy pants worn tight from the knee down, and low-heeled leather boots.

The black hat soon became a lauhala (pandanus) one, often adorned with "cowboy leis" fashioned from vines and flowers found in the forests. Paniolo, after spending time in the wilderness, even decorated their horses with sweet-smelling vines.

The pansy lei of Waimea, for example, is credited to an early paniolo, an Irishman named Jack Purdy, who married a part-Hawaiian woman named Fanny Davis. Purdy cultivated pansy seeds, which grew into the flower Hawaiians call puapoʻokanaka. The pansy lei became a favorite of Big Island paniolo.

By the 1840s, it had become too difficult to keep up with the demand for beef by rounding up wild longhorns. Privately owned domestic herds were easier and more profitable. The Great Mahele, a grand but often mis-guided attempt to allot land for private ownership, allowed for the creation of the first large cattle ranches in the islands.

The beef industry grew steadily, but slowly, along with the crops of sugar and pineapple. Most of the old ranches were located in the cooler uplands—ranches like Parker, Kahuā, Huʻehuʻe, McCandless, Puʻuwaʻawaʻa, Haleakalā, ʻUlupalakua, Molokaʻi, and Kaupō.

The old ranches face tough new challenges today, but the tradition of the paniolo is still alive at most of them.

Fish and Their Friends

Since Hawai'i is an island state, located smack in the middle of the Pacific, fish is, understandably, a mainstay on island tables. The following is a guide to help you recreate the recipes in this book with the freshest fish from your area.

Hawaiian fish fall into four categories: tuna, billfish, open-ocean fish, and bottom fish. The state of Hawai'i has been encouraging the use of fish other than the already popular 'ahi and mahimahi, and has for several years given professional chefs and home cooks more information on other species.

'Ahi (bigeye tuna/yellowfin tuna)— These two species are both known in Hawai'i as 'ahi. The peak season for fishing 'ahi is during the winter months from October through April. It is clearly one of Hawai'i's favorite fish, used most often in fresh sashimi and poke. It tastes like steak when marinated and barbecued, and can be fried, poached, or used in fish stews. 'Ahi is the mildest and lightest of the tuna species. Substitutions: bluefin or blackfin tuna.

Aku (skipjack tuna)—Aku is a Pacific tuna that moves into Hawaiian waters in abundance from April through September. The meat is red and stronger in flavor than most white-meat fish. Hawaiians like it raw in poke, or as sashimi, and pan fried. Aku is also a fish of Hawaiian legends. In old Hawai'i, to honor the fish, several days a year old people were not allowed to eat it. Substitutions: any small tuna or bonito.

A'u or kajiki (Pacific blue marlin)—A'u is larger and has a heavier bill than other marlin commonly caught in island waters. All marlin is lean and must not be overcooked. It works best fried, poached, or marinated and grilled. It is most plentiful in summer and fall (June through October). A'u has white meat and is often seen as the Catch of the Day on restaurant menus. Nairagi and shutome are two other types of marlin in Hawai'i markets. Substitutions: swordfish or thresher shark.

Kūmū (goatfish)—Kūmū is a reef fish with delicate, mild meat. It can be caught

year round and is not often supplied to restaurants and markets in great numbers. Kūmū is often fried in butter with lemon and garlic or steamed and served with a sauce. Be careful not to overcook. Substitutions: any white-meat fish with high fat content.

Mahimahi (dolphinfish or dorado)— "Mahi" is by far the most well known island fish. It is favored for its mild, sweet flavor and versatility. Although it's available most of the year, it peaks during the months from March to May and September to November. It is thin-skinned and firm with light pink flesh. Mahimahi should be cooked only until it flakes and not a second longer. A favorite preparation is simply to sauté it in lemon and butter. Substitutions: halibut, catfish, black cod, flounder, perch.

Onaga (red snapper or 'ula'ula)—Onaga is one of Hawai'i's most important bottom fish. It is caught mostly in the fall and winter months. Because it has a shorter shelf life than fish such as 'ōpakapaka, it is not sold as often in the fresh market. It has white-pink flesh and is moist and sweet. Onaga makes some of the best winter sashimi. It is also good baked or steamed. Onaga heads are popular for making soup. Substitutions: halibut, sole, turbot, rock cod, flounder.

'Ono (wahoo)—'Ono is a relative of the mackerel; however, its meat is pale white and its flavor sweet. Not especially abundant in Hawaiian waters, it can be caught primarily in the summer and fall. 'Ono is often a substitute on menus for mahimahi. However, mahimahi is more moist. Do not overcook this fish. It is best quick fried, or poached with a sauce. Substitutions: haddock, halibut, swordfish.

Opah (moonfish)—Opah is a colorful, roundish fish with large eyes that usually hangs out with tunas and billfish. It is available mostly from April through August, but never in large numbers. It is an underutilized fish that is often used when other more popular species are not available. Its flesh is rich and fatty and can be broiled and smoked or used for sashimi. Substitutions: any large-grained fish with rich and creamy flesh.

ʻŌpakapaka (pink snapper)—ʻŌpakapaka is a highly popular fish on restaurant menus. It can be caught year round, but peaks during the winter months. ʻŌpakapaka is now often exported whole to a growing market on the U.S. mainland. It has a clear, light flesh and a firm texture, as well as a delicate flavor. It is most often prepared by steaming or baking. Other well-suited preparations are poaching and sautéing. Substitutions: black cod, flounder, lingcod, ocean perch, sole, turbot.

Ulua (pompano)—Ulua belongs to the trevally family of fish. When it is large (over 10 pounds and up to 100), it's an "ulua"; under 10 pounds it's called "papio." The smaller papio are often sold whole in fish markets, while the larger ulua are marketed in filets and chunks. Ulua's firm, white flesh

makes it ideal for almost any method of cooking. Substitutions: any fish with firm white meat.

61

TIPS ON HANDLING FRESH FISH

Always keep fish in the coldest part of your refrigerator. Lean fish will keep longer than fatty fish, but count on keeping it for no more than two or three days.

Sometimes you cannot eat your fresh fish right away and must freeze it. The sooner you freeze it after it is caught, the more likely it is to retain its fresh qualities, since bacteria has not begun to spread.

Do not freeze fish you purchased at a market unless you are certain it hasn't already been frozen once before you purchased it.

You can get rid of strong, "fishy" odors (make sure the odors aren't caused by spoilage) by wiping the pieces with lemon juice to help reduce bacteria. Another method is to soak the fish in tomato juice or cook it in a tomato-based sauce.

'AHI MISO BURGER

Serves 4

'Ahi is the darling of the stylish restaurant set. Here is a simpler way to prepare an 'ahi burger. If you're a more hardcore fish lover, you can use aku.

1	pound 'ahi, chopped
$1/2$	cup chopped round onion
1	stalk green onion, finely chopped
1	clove garlic, minced
1	egg
$1/2$	cup miso
	Juice of $1/2$ lime
	Salt and pepper to taste
	Peanut oil for frying

Cut away the blood meat of the fish and any skin. Use the filet only, and chop to resemble hamburger. In a bowl, mix the green onion, garlic, egg, miso, and lime juice. Form into patties. In a skillet over medium-high heat, heat the oil and fry the patties until crisp and brown on both sides. Season to taste. Drain on paper towels. Keep warm until ready to serve.

OPAH WITH PLUM WINE SAUCE

Serves 4

Opah, or moonfish, was until recently caught by longline fishermen on the open ocean and given away as a gesture of goodwill. It is a large-grained, fatty fish that cooks to a white color and is available mostly in the spring and summer. This recipe is from chef OnJin Kim of the former Hanatei Bistro in Hawai'i Kai.

3	ounces crabmeat
2	teaspoons mayonnaise
2	teaspoons green onion, finely sliced
4	5-ounce opah filets
	Salt and pepper
1	tablespoon butter

Plum Wine Sauce:

1	cup Japanese plum wine
2	minced shallots
1	bay leaf
$1/2$	teaspoon white peppercorns
2	cups whipping cream
$1/4$	pound softened butter
1	2-ounce can lychees, drained
1	tablespoon butter

Preheat the oven to 350 degrees F. Separate the crabmeat and mix with mayonnaise and green onion. Cut a pocket in each opah filet and fill with crab mix. Season with salt and pepper. In a skillet over medium-high heat, melt the butter and sear the fish on both sides. Place in the oven for 5 minutes to finish cooking.

To make the sauce: Combine the wine, shallots, bay leaf, and peppercorns in a saucepan over medium heat. Bring to a boil and reduce until about 2 tablespoons of liquid remains. Add the cream and reduce by one-third. Whisk in the $1/4$ pound butter in bits. Strain and keep warm. In a skillet over medium heat, sauté the lychees in 1 tablespoon butter. Mix in the wine sauce and heat. Serve over the opah filets.

PANKO FRIED ULUA

Serves 4

This recipe will work well with any fresh fish with firm white meat. Panko is a breading available in Asian markets. You will love its crispy, crunchy character when fried.

1	cup flour
4	ulua filets
1	egg, well beaten
1/2	cup milk
4	tablespoons butter
1	cup panko breadcrumbs
2	tablespoons lemon juice
2	tablespoons capers
	Salt to taste
4	tablespoons butter
1	clove garlic, minced

Lightly flour the ulua. Combine egg and milk and dip fish in the mixture. Roll the fish in the panko. Sauté in butter until the outside is light brown and crisp. The fish will flake easily. Do not overcook. Make a sauce by warming the lemon juice, capers, and salt. Whip the 4 tablespoons butter with the minced garlic and add to the sauce. Allow the butter to just melt. Pour over the fish and serve immediately.

POACHED ONAGA IN SAKE SAUCE

Serves 6

Onaga, uku, and 'ōpakapaka are all Hawaiian names of fish in the snapper family (red, gray, and pink snapper). Their meat is moist, mild, and highly desirable for poaching, steaming, and baking. Always buy the freshest fish you can find in your area. This dish can be prepared quickly and served with hot rice and a vegetable.

2	cups water
2/3	cup shoyu
2	tablespoons sake or dry white wine
1/2	cup sugar
1/4	cup green onion, chopped, with green tops
1	tablespoon ginger, peeled and minced
2	pounds onaga filets

Combine all ingredients except the onaga. Place in a large skillet and bring to a boil. Reduce the sauce to simmer and place filets in pan. Cover and simmer for 10 minutes or until fish is done. Remove fish, place on a platter, and keep warm. Bring the pan juices to a boil and cook for another 10 minutes. Pour reduced sauce over the fish.

Seared 'Ahi with Miso Sauce

Serves 6

Seared 'ahi is one of those dishes that have come to define Hawaiian regional cuisine. On the mainland 'ahi is marketed as yellowfin or albacore tuna and is often found as sashimi in Japanese sushi bars. 'Ahi can also be marinated and grilled.

3	tablespoons cooking oil
12	ounces (2 blocks) sashimi-grade 'ahi, or thick 'ahi steaks

Miso Sauce:

4	tablespoons miso (bean paste)
$^1/_2$	cup Japanese rice vinegar
2	tablespoons Korean hot sauce (ko choo jang)
2	tablespoons green onion, chopped
2	tablespoons honey
2	teaspoons fresh ginger, finely minced
2	teaspoons sesame oil
	White sesame seeds to garnish

Heat the oil in a skillet until very hot and sear the block of 'ahi on all four sides until the outside is cooked and the center remains pink and raw (only about 20 seconds on each side). Drain on paper towels and cool. You may also wrap the 'ahi in plastic wrap and place in the freezer while you prepare the sauce. This will firm it up and make it easier to slice. If block sashimi 'ahi is not available, use the thickest 'ahi steaks you can find and sear on two sides for approximately 15 seconds.

Prepare miso sauce by mixing together the miso, vinegar, and hot sauce until smooth. Then add the onion, honey, ginger, and sesame oil. To serve, spoon the sauce onto a platter, slice the 'ahi, and arrange on top of the vinaigrette. Garnish with sesame seeds.

KA LEI: THE SYMBOL OF ALOHA AND WELCOME

Lei in some form can be found in virtually all the cultures of the world, from the tribal villages of Indonesia to the drawing rooms of England, where a strand of pearls becomes a lei. But nowhere has the art of the lei, a symbol of welcome and love, been so elevated and developed as in Hawaiʻi.

It's believed that the first lei came with the early Tahitian settlers. Lei maile (Alyxia olivaeformis), hala (pandanus fruit), hinahina (Heliotropium anomalum), and ferns are used throughout the Pacific, as are lei of shells.

In pre-contact Hawaiʻi and on through the early 1900s, certain lei were reserved only for aliʻi (royalty). The lei palaoa, made of coils of human hair attached to olonā cord with a hook-shaped pendant of ivory, for instance, was reserved only for the ruling classes. The lei hulu, or feather lei, was worn primarily by the women of chiefly rank.

The lei was a symbol of esteem for everyone from gods to family and self. Lei were laid at altars of the hula, farming, and fishing—and adorned the average person just for the sheer joy in the wearing. Today, lei are given freely at all occasions and are worn with pride and enjoyment.

Hawaiian men are never embarrassed by wearing flowers. The paniolo, or Hawaiian cowboys, have always set their own lei style by making hasty leis for their hats and horses from available shrubbery. You could always tell where a paniolo had been watching the cattle by the contents of his lei.

In bygone days, cowboys from different islands were known for specific lei—for instance, the pansy became known as a "Waimea lei." The cowboys of ʻUlupalakua and Upcountry Maui were known for their lei ʻākulikuli (a coastal herb with small white and magenta flowers), and lei lokelani (Damask and China roses). On Moloka'i, the paniolo lei was made of roses and mei sui lan (a fragrant flower introduced from China).

In 1928, largely due to the urging of island poet and promoter Don Blanding and the support of several island businesses, the first Lei Day was celebrated on May 1. Territorial Governor Wallace R. Farrington officially proclaimed it so, saying, "Thus, the world at large may know the flowering season is welcome and our own people will be happier for their part in broadcasting the spirit of aloha."

Through the years, May Day as Lei Day has survived especially well in the schools. There it remains a celebration of aloha, affection, and international unity.

Vegetables and Backyard Produce

When I began thinking of doing a book on island cuisine, it was the backyard produce that interested me the most. At the time, I lived in a house near downtown Honolulu with a beautiful old breadfruit tree in the front yard. Even though I had been served breadfruit while growing up, the trees themselves had disappeared except in remote communities, and I hadn't the slightest idea what to do when faced with the whole, fresh fruit, with its rough outer skin and sappy stem. It occurred to me that the preparation of breadfruit, as well as other once common island produce, was something to explore.

Mango chutney was another thing I had grown up with. Both grandmothers made it every mango season from May through September. There were always several jars in our refrigerator, and no one ever thought of going to the store to actually purchase some. The homemade variety has become harder and harder to find as backyard mango trees in old neighborhoods become scarcer. Making chutney—once a nice way to spend an afternoon with friends—has become a luxury as a result of busy schedules and two-career families.

One of my most vivid grade school memories is of standing at the back door of the Kaunoa School cafeteria in Spreckelsville, Maui, excitedly waiting for a paper cone cup filled with sweet-sour prune "mui" or "crack seed." The cafeteria ladies, cheerful and scrubbed in their starched white uniforms, would mix it up on their own and sell it to us for a nickel during recess.

Crack seed, or preserved plums, peaches, and other fruit, came to Hawai'i originally from China, and has been enjoyed for generations by both children and adults.

One of the earliest and best known import companies is Honolulu's Yick Lung Co. However, the prune version of crack seed was made at home until recently because it was less expensive, and there were times, such as during World War II, when it was not available.

Here are ideas for using up that backyard produce given you by friends. Maybe you'll even find a recipe for something you've long since forgotten.

AUNTIE ROBBIE'S PRUNE CRACK SEED

Makes 1 gallon

Auntie Robbie St. Sure Apana always made her prune mui in large gallon mayonnaise jars for her children, nieces and nephews, and all the neighborhood children. She watched for packaged prunes and dried fruits such as apricots to go on sale at the local markets. The Chinese dried lemon peel and li hing mui (salty dried plums) are available in Asian markets where candy and snacks are sold.

1	pound dark brown sugar
3	tablespoons Hawaiian rock salt or kosher salt
3	tablespoons bourbon
1	tablespoon Chinese Five Spice powder
2	cups fresh lemon juice
8	12-ounce packages pitted prunes
2	12-ounce packages dried apricots or mixed dried fruit
$1/2$	pound Chinese dried lemon peel, cut into small pieces
$1/2$	pound seedless li hing mui

In a large bowl, combine sugar, salt, bourbon, Five Spice, and lemon juice. Toss in prunes and other dried fruit, lemon peel, and li hing mui. Place in a clean gallon jar to soak. Let stand for a minimum of 4 days, mixing twice a day.

NUTTY BAKED BREADFRUIT

Serves 6 to 8

When preparing breadfruit, remember to oil your hands first and wear old clothing, as it can stain.

1	whole breadfruit (starting to soften) Water
$1/4$	cup raisins
$1/4$	cup chopped macadamia nuts
6	tablespoons butter
3	tablespoons honey Ground cinnamon and nutmeg to taste
1	cup coconut milk

Preheat the oven to 350 degrees F. The breadfruit should still be firm enough to cut in half. Remove the stem and inner core. Peel the outer skin. Slice the breadfruit meat into $1/2$-inch pieces and place in a baking dish. Fill dish, covering the breadfruit with enough water to measure 1 inch. Sprinkle the raisins, nuts, and butter over the top. Drizzle the honey on top of that. Sprinkle with cinnamon and nutmeg. Cover with coconut milk. Cover the top of the dish with aluminum foil. Bake for 1 hour.

GUAVA KETCHUP

Makes 2 quarts

Guava season is from June to October. Guava was brought to Hawai'i from South America in the early 1800s and soon grew wild along the roadsides and in pastures. This ketchup is a local classic.

3	quarts guava pulp*
5	medium onions, sliced
$^1/_4$	cup water
2	cloves garlic, sliced
5	small red chili peppers, chopped
2	cups white vinegar
4	teaspoons ground allspice
3	teaspoons ground cinnamon
2	teaspoons ground cloves
6	cups sugar
	Salt to taste

*Prepare the guava pulp by peeling and halving the fruit and removing the seeds. Place in an aluminum or stainless steel saucepan. Add enough water to cover the guava. Bring to a boil and cook until soft, about 10 minutes. Cool. Put through a sieve or food mill, or process in a food processor with a small amount of water to make a thick purée.

Place guava purée and all other ingredients in a saucepan and simmer over low heat for 30 to 40 minutes. Pour into hot sterilized jars and seal immediately.

Kinau Wilder's Mango Chutney

Makes 10 pints

Kinau Wilder, born into one of Hawai'i's most prestigious kama'āina families, was a beauty and an actress in her youth, an entrepreneur in early Waikīkī nightspots in midlife, a delightful hostess always, and finally a mender of fine china par excellence. She made batches of this chutney to give to friends and relatives. According to Maili Yardley, Kinau pronounced it, without reservation or false pride, "the best chutney ever made!" This chutney is baked instead of cooked on top of the stove, and its origins can be traced to Hawai'i's early missionary families.

24	cups sliced fresh mangoes
5	pounds raw sugar (these sugar crystals have a molasses flavor)
1	1-pound box seedless raisins
1	handful Hawaiian rock salt, or kosher salt
1	head of garlic, peeled and minced
1	pint white vinegar
15	small red Hawaiian chili peppers
1	hand fresh ginger, or 5 pieces the size of your thumb
1	teaspoon ground cinnamon
1	teaspoon nutmeg
1	teaspoon allspice
1	teaspoon ground cloves
1	tablespoon mustard seed
3	finely sliced lemons, with seeds removed

Preheat the oven to 375 degrees F. Peel and chop mangoes. Mix mangoes with raw sugar, raisins, and salt and place in a roasting pan. Put garlic, vinegar, chili peppers, and ginger in a blender or food processor and chop up. Add spices and lemons and mix. Combine with the mango mixture. Roast for 3 hours, stirring occasionally and checking to make sure it doesn't dry out. Add water as needed. Place in sterilized jars, process, and store. (See page 7 for processing instructions.)

LYCHEE SHERBET

Makes 1 quart

If you're not lucky enough to have access to a lychee tree, substitute the canned variety.

1	cup lychee juice (made from 20 or so lychees)
1	tablespoon gelatin
$1/4$	cup cold water
$2/3$	cup milk
$1/2$	cup sugar
1	cup cream
1	teaspoon lemon juice

Peel the hard outer shell of the lychees and remove the seeds. Wrap the fruit in a piece of cheesecloth and squeeze to remove the juice. You should get about 1 cup. Place the gelatin in a bowl and sprinkle with the cold water. Allow to stand 5 minutes. In a saucepan, scald $1/3$ cup of the milk, add the gelatin, and stir until dissolved. Add the sugar, mix well, and cool. Add the remaining $1/3$ cup milk, cream, lychee juice, and lemon juice. Process with an ice cream maker according to directions.

PAPAYA-PINEAPPLE MARMALADE

Makes $2^1/2$ quarts

I had almost forgotten how common this combination of tastes once was in Hawaiian kitchens until I was reminded by island chef Sam Choy, a generous man who has taken humble home cooking and turned it into fine island cuisine. In the days when more people made jams and jellies at home, they used them liberally on everything from toast to vanilla ice cream and as a glaze for roasted chicken. If the fresh fruit is not available, use canned. However, fresh is best.

10	cups firm ripe papaya, chopped
1	cup fresh pineapple, chopped
1	orange
2	lemons
3	tablespoons grated fresh ginger
$1/2$	teaspoon salt
5 to 7	cups sugar

Combine papaya and pineapple in a large saucepan. Grate the orange and lemon rinds. Squeeze 1 cup of juice from the orange and lemons. Add juice, rinds, ginger, and salt to the papaya and pineapple. Bring to a boil. Reduce the heat and continue cooking for 30 minutes. Add sugar and taste. Add more if mixture is not sweet enough. Cook another 30 minutes, stirring to avoid burning. Pour jam into sterilized jars and seal. Keeps up to 6 months.

SPICY BAKED PAPAYA

Serves 6

Papaya is usually enjoyed chilled for breakfast, but this version is a nice change, as well as an excellent accompaniment to curry or leg of lamb. Here we bake the papaya halves; however, you may want to peel, seed, and slice them into a casserole to serve at a buffet. Allow one half papaya per person.

3	medium-sized ripe papayas
2	tablespoons butter, cut into 6 equal slices
	Squeeze of lemon
	Dash to taste of ground cinnamon and nutmeg

Preheat the oven to 350 degrees F. Cut the papaya in half and remove seed. Place halves in an ovenproof baking dish and place a slice of butter in each. Top with a squeeze of lemon (or lime) and season with cinnamon and nutmeg. Bake for 10 minutes or until easily pierced with a fork. Do not let the papaya get mushy. Serve immediately.

TARO AU GRATIN

Serves 6

Taro gets "dressed up" here and is fancy enough for company dinner.

3	cups taro, cooked and diced
6	tablespoons butter
$2^1/_4$	cups milk or heavy cream
$4^1/_2$	tablespoons flour
	Salt to taste
$^1/_2$	cup grated Cheddar or Jack cheese
$^1/_4$	cup breadcrumbs

Preheat the oven to 375 degrees F. Prepare the taro by scrubbing the corm, placing in a saucepan, and covering with water. Cover and boil for about $1^1/_2$ hours, or until tender. Remove and cool. Peel and slice the taro into rounds. In a saucepan, over medium heat, melt 5 tablespoons butter and add the flour. Stir until smooth, then add the milk or cream gradually to make a sauce. Cook until the mixture thickens. Season with salt. In an oiled baking dish, arrange the taro slices, sauce, and cheese in alternate layers. Melt the remaining 1 tablespoon butter and mix with the breadcrumbs. Sprinkle on top of the layered taro. Bake for 30 minutes, or until the taro is heated through and the crumbs are browned.

PALAKA: PLANTATIONS TO POLITICS

A few years ago, my teenage son, who was attending a Maui high school, was sent home with a demerit slip for wearing a non-Hawaiian shirt on Aloha Friday. His teacher, obviously not from Hawai'i, declared that his palaka shirt simply did not qualify as an aloha shirt.

It made me angry enough to shoot back to school a note saying that a shirt of palaka probably had more significance for Hawai'i than one of those silly rayon numbers with palm trees created for tourists in the 1940s. Palaka, a cotton twill with characteristic blue-and-white block print woven into the fabric rather than printed, has over the years become a symbol of "localness."

The fabric was introduced to Hawai'i in the early 1800s by whalers, who brought it from New England. The "Cranston," or "Sturbridge," plaid is often found in the northeastern United States used as upholstery fabric.

Peter Young Kaeo, an inmate at the leprosy settlement at Kalaupapa in 1873, wrote his cousin, Queen Emma, saying he had purchased several yards of cotton twill "to make me some frocks Palaka."

The word "palaka" is thought to have been a transliteration of the word "block." However, Kaeo's letter suggests it was a Hawaiianized version of the word "frock," meaning a loose-fitting man's shirt without tails, made of a sturdy material.

The popularity of palaka really took hold during the early sugar-and-pineapple-growing period of the late 1800s because it was strong and could protect the immigrant workers from the cutting edges of the cane and pine. For Japanese laborers, it was close to their own "kasuri" fabric. Palaka was often used by immigrant Scots as a work uniform. Many of them were mill engineers and accountants on plantations, and the fabric resembled their own Scottish plaid.

Soon Hawaiian paniolo began using palaka for their rough-riding ranch work. During the 1920s and 1930s it became a household word.

In the mid-1970s, a young University of Hawai'i Law School graduate named David Hagino brought the concept of palaka into island politics with a twenty-two–page pamphlet he called "Palaka Power." The pamphlet suggested an ordering of priorities by the new State Constitutional Convention in the summer of 1978. Hagino and his friends, one of whom was a young man named John Waihee (who later became Hawai'i's governor), wanted to cement state power in local hands.

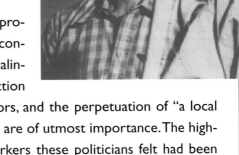

Palaka Power stood for a strong pro-union attitude, the limiting of growth by conserving fuel and water while banning desalinization plants and nuclear power, the rejection of initiative, elected judges and prosecutors, and the perpetuation of "a local value system," in which family and friends are of utmost importance. The highly symbolic plaid, worn by plantation workers these politicians felt had been oppressed, was the perfect rallying cloth.

Many now feel disillusioned by the failure of "Palaka Power." At its best, it called for the different interest groups that make up Hawai'i to band together to promote the interests of the common people.

Palaka can take its place as a Hawaiian classic.

6

Desserts, Cakes, and Breads

Islanders have a natural sweet tooth. Fruit and custards are often added to cakes such as haupia (coconut pudding) and guava. Then there are the comforting, old-timey desserts like fruit cobblers and crisps, tapioca puddings, and pineapple upside-down cakes—desserts that were once typical in island families.

Festival goodies from different ethnic groups have made it into the mainstream of island life. Treats such as Japanese manju (flaky bean cakes) or mochi cakes at New Year's and sugary Filipino cascaron (coconut mochi fritters) on sticks at county fairs are well-loved throughout Hawai'i.

Almost as well-loved by islanders as Portuguese bean soup are the sweet bread and malassadas (doughnuts) brought in originally as special-occasion desserts by the Portuguese. Sweet bread is a perfect accompaniment to the soup. In earlier times it was made only on special occasions such as Easter and First Holy Communion. Malassadas are doughnuts much like the beignets of New Orleans. The Portuguese traditionally made them on Fat or Shrove Tuesday, the day before Ash Wednesday and the Lenten season.

ACADEMY CAFE CHOCOLATE SAUCE

Makes about 3 cups

One of the loveliest spots in Honolulu to lunch is the courtyard restaurant at the Honolulu Academy of Arts.

1	16-ounce can of chocolate fudge topping
8	ounces chocolate syrup
1/2	teaspoon cinnamon
	Salt to taste
4	tablespoons Kahlua liqueur or creme de cacao
	Candied ginger for topping

In a medium bowl, mix all the ingredients together until well blended. Refrigerate until ready to serve. Serve on vanilla ice cream with chopped candied ginger.

CASCARON

Makes 1 dozen

This chewy coconut fritter is a favorite at island bazaars and fairs. The fritters, which are Filipino in origin, are usually threaded on bamboo barbecue sticks for easy eating.

	Oil for deep frying
1	package mochiko flour
1	14-ounce package sweetened coconut, flaked
4	cups water
1	cup sugar
1/2	cup or more honey

Heat the oil in a deep fryer or skillet to about 350 degrees F. In a bowl, mix the mochiko flour, coconut, water, and sugar together. Shape the dough into 1^1/$_2$-inch balls and deep fry until golden brown. Be careful not to let the balls stick to each other. Drain the fritters on absorbent paper towels and drizzle with honey. If you choose, you can thread the coconut balls onto wooden barbecue sticks.

CARAMELIZED BANANAS WITH RUM SAUCE AND VANILLA ICE CREAM

Serves 4

Apple bananas are particularly good in this recipe. Serve warm over vanilla ice cream.

3	tablespoons unsalted butter
2	apple bananas, not too ripe, cut into 1-inch pieces
1/4	cup plus 2 tablespoons brown sugar
1/2	cup light rum
1	pint vanilla ice cream

In a skillet over medium heat, melt the butter and 1/4 cup sugar. Add the bananas and sauté until they just turn brown, about 3 minutes. Sprinkle the remaining 2 tablespoons of sugar over the bananas and cook until sugar melts, about another 3 minutes. Remove from the heat and pour rum into the skillet. Ignite with a match and let the flames die out. Place the ice cream into 4 bowls and spoon the bananas over it. Serve immediately.

CHINESE ALMOND FLOAT

Serves 4 to 6

When you want something light and fruity to clear your palate after a rich dinner, this colorful dessert fits the bill.

1 1/2	envelopes unflavored gelatin
1/3	cup cold water
1	cup boiling water
1/2	cup sugar
1/2	cup evaporated skim milk
3/4	teaspoon almond extract
1	15-ounce can lychees
1	small can mandarin oranges
1/2	cup fresh mango or papaya
1/2	cup seedless grapes

In a bowl, soften the gelatin in the cold water. Add the boiling water and sugar and stir until the sugar is dissolved. Add the evaporated milk and almond extract and mix well. Pour the mixture into an 8-inch-square baking pan. Chill in the refrigerator until set. When set, cut into 1-inch squares. In a large bowl, mix the lychee and oranges, including the syrup from the cans, mango, papaya, and grapes. Gently mix in the almond squares. Serve chilled in bowls.

CHOCOLATE MINT BARS

Makes 3 dozen

Try this using top-quality Hawaiian Vintage Chocolate for a special treat.

1	6-ounce package chocolate pieces
1	cup butter
1³/₄	cup graham cracker crumbs
1	cup flaked coconut
¹/₂	cup macadamia nuts, chopped
2	8-ounce packages cream cheese
1	cup sifted powdered sugar
¹/₂	teaspoon mint extract
	Few drops green food coloring, optional

In a saucepan over low heat, melt ¹/₃ cup of the chocolate with ³/₄ cup of the butter, stirring until smooth. Add the crumbs, coconut, and nuts. Mix well. Press onto the bottom of an ungreased 9- x 13-inch baking pan. Chill. In a bowl, combine the softened cream cheese, powdered sugar, mint extract, and food coloring, mixing until well blended. Spread the mixture over the crust. Chill. In a saucepan over low heat, melt the remaining chocolate pieces with the remaining butter. Stir until smooth. Spread the chocolate mixture over the cream cheese layer. Chill until firm. Cut into bars and serve chilled.

FRESH MULBERRY PIE

Serves 6

My mother almost never cooked, which is why I remember to this day the mulberry pie she and our maid, Aggie, made from the berries we kids gathered in the lot next door.

Double crust pie crust:

2	cups sifted flour
1	teaspoon salt
1	cup shortening (such as Crisco)
5 to 6	tablespoons cold water

Filling:

1	cup sugar
4	tablespoons flour
	Salt to taste
3	cups mulberries
1	tablespoon lemon juice

Preheat the oven to 450 degrees F. Make the pie crust by sifting the flour and salt together into a bowl. Cut in the shortening until the mixture resembles peas or rice. Stirring with a fork, add enough cold water to moisten the flour mixture. Form the dough into 2 balls. On a floured board or pastry cloth, roll out the first ball with a rolling pin. Fold in half twice while rolling. Fit the pastry into the bottom of a 9-inch pie pan.

For filling, in a bowl, combine the sugar, flour, and salt. Place about a $1/4$ of the mixture in the bottom of the unbaked shell. Add the berries and top with the remaining sugar and flour mixture. Sprinkle top with lemon juice. Roll out the second pastry ball for the top crust and cover the pie. Tuck the ends of the crust and trim. Cut slits for steam in the top crust. Bake for 10 minutes. Reduce the heat to 350 degrees and continue to bake another 30 minutes, or until crust is golden. Remove and cool.

HAUPIA

Serves 6

This simple coconut pudding is served at lū'au and used as a filling for cakes and breads.

2	tablespoons cornstarch
3	tablespoons sugar
$1/8$	teaspoon salt
2	cups coconut milk

In a bowl, make a smooth paste of the cornstarch, sugar, salt, and 1 cup of the coconut milk. In a saucepan over low heat, scald the remaining 1 cup milk, stirring constantly. Add the cornstarch mixture and continue to cook until it thickens to a translucent color and coats the spoon. Pour the mixture into a shallow pan. Refrigerate until firm. Cut into squares and serve on pieces of trimmed ti leaves.

HŌLUALOA INN'S SWEET BREAD FRENCH TOAST

Serves 8

Hōlualoa Inn is a lovely bed-and-breakfast spot in Kona's coffee-growing region. This French toast is rich and custardlike. Punaluʻu brand sweet bread is baked in a rectangular loaf and slices easily. This shape works better than the bun shape.

8	slices Punaluʻu Portuguese sweet bread
1	stick butter, softened
1	teaspoon or more ground cinnamon
5	eggs
3	egg yolks
$1/2$	cup honey
1	can evaporated milk
$2 1/2$	teaspoons vanilla
4	cups whole milk
	Grated coconut, macadamia nuts, and crushed pineapple for toppings

Slice the sweet bread into slices about 1 inch thick and spread with butter on both sides. Lay the slices flat in a 9- x 13-inch glass baking pan. Sprinkle with cinnamon. Preheat the oven to 300 degrees F. In a blender, mix the eggs, egg yolks, honey, evaporated milk, vanilla, and whole milk until just blended. This can be done the night before. Pour the egg mixture over the bread slices. Bake for 45 minutes, or until the slices puff up and a knife inserted comes out clean. Top the slices with shredded coconut, macadamia nuts, and crushed pineapple.

KONA COFFEE CRYSTAL CAKE

Serves 8 to 10

This cake is made using instant coffee crystals. It tastes better when it has had a chance to "rest" after baking.

$^1/_2$	cup oil
$^1/_3$	cup sugar
1	stick butter, melted
4	eggs, beaten
1	8-ounce container sour cream
1	box yellow cake mix (without pudding)
2	tablespoons instant coffee crystals

Glaze:

1	tablespoon butter or margarine
2	tablespoons fresh lime juice
$^3/_4$	cup powdered sugar
1	tablespoon water

Preheat the oven to 325 degrees F. In a large mixing bowl, combine the oil, sugar, melted butter, eggs, sour cream, and cake mix. Add the coffee crystals and mix together. Pour into a greased 9- x 13-inch cake pan. Bake for 40 to 45 minutes, or until cake pulls away from the sides of the pan. Make the glaze by melting the butter in a saucepan and adding the lime juice, powdered sugar, and water. Pour the glaze over the warm cake and cool.

MALASSADAS

Makes 3 dozen

The "eggy" dough and the use of evaporated milk make malassadas different from other types of doughnuts. Some say that real malassadas must be made with potato flour or by adding mashed potatoes to the dough. Others add a pinch of nutmeg or vanilla flavoring. This recipe does not include those ingredients.

$3/4$	teaspoon salt
3	cups flour
$1/4$	cup sugar
$1/2$	cup boiling water
2	tablespoons butter
$1/2$	cup canned evaporated milk
4	eggs, beaten
1	package yeast (about 1 tablespoon)
$1/4$	cup warm water for yeast
	Oil for deep frying
	Granulated sugar for coating

In a large bowl, sift together the salt, flour, and sugar. In a saucepan over medium-high heat, bring the $1/2$ cup water to a boil and dissolve the butter in it. Remove from heat. Add the milk to the water and butter. Mix the sifted salt, flour, and sugar with the milk mixture. Add the beaten eggs. Dissolve the yeast in the $1/4$ cup lukewarm water and add to the mixture. Blend well. Place in a clean, oiled bowl, cover with a cloth, and allow to rise in a warm place, out of a draft, until double in size. Heat enough oil for deep frying in a large saucepan or deep fryer. Test to see if the oil is hot enough by dropping a small amount of dough into it. When the dough rises quickly to the top and sizzles briskly, the oil is ready. Drop the dough by the heaping teaspoonful into the hot oil and brown on all sides. Remove and drain on a brown paper bag or absorbent paper towels. While the doughnuts are still warm, roll them in sugar, or shake them in a bag with a small amount of sugar. Serve warm with cold milk or hot coffee.

OLD-FASHIONED COCONUT CANDY

Makes about 12 pieces

During the heyday of the plantations, sweets were harder to come by than today, and many people made this simple candy in their home kitchens. If you prefer, brown sugar can be used instead of white.

2   cups grated fresh coconut
2   cups sugar
     Water to moisten

Grate fresh coconut (see pages 5–6) or use the unsweetened canned variety. In a saucepan over medium heat, cook the sugar with just enough water to moisten well. Cook until the mixture threads from the spoon. Add the grated coconut and mix. Continue to cook for 10 minutes, stirring frequently. Remove from stove and test a small portion by beating it with a spoon. If the candy creams and hardens quickly when dropped on a piece of waxed paper, it's ready. Otherwise, return the pot to the stove briefly and test again. When the mixture passes the test, beat thoroughly and drop onto oiled paper. Cool and store in an airtight container between pieces of waxed paper, or wrap individually.

POI DOUGHNUTS

Makes 4 dozen

The mochiko flour and ready-made poi give these doughnuts a wonderful texture and make them simple to prepare.

          Oil for frying
1   12-ounce bag of poi
2   10-ounce packages mochiko flour
$1^1/_2$ cups sugar
2   cups water
          Sugar for coating

In a deep skillet or dutch oven, heat about 1 inch of cooking oil to about 300 degrees F. In a bowl, mix the poi, mochiko flour, sugar, and water until blended. Drop by the teaspoonful into the hot oil and fry until golden brown on all sides. Drain on absorbent paper towels and roll in sugar.

RIPE BREADFRUIT PUDDING

Serves 4 to 6

An unimaginably rich, custardy pudding

1	ripe breadfruit, soft and brown
1	cup sugar
	Cinnamon to taste
	Salt to taste
$1^1/_2$	cups coconut milk

Preheat the oven to 350 degrees F. To prepare breadfruit, pull out the stem, cut in half, and take out the core. Scrape out the soft pulp meat. It will make about 3 cups of pulp. Add sugar, cinnamon, and salt to the pulp and mix well. Blend in the coconut milk until mixed. Oil an ovenproof baking dish and pour the mixture into it. Bake for 1 hour, or until pudding sets. Serve warm with more coconut milk or cream.

RUM PUDDING CAKE

Serves 8 to 10

I actually prefer this cake the next day, when the flavors have combined and it seems more moist.

$^1/_2$	cup slivered almonds
1	18-ounce box yellow cake mix
1	package instant vanilla pudding mix
$^1/_2$	cup water
$^1/_2$	cup white rum
$^1/_2$	cup oil
4	eggs

Glaze:

$^1/_2$	cup sugar
1	stick butter
$^1/_4$	cup dark rum
$^1/_4$	cup water

Preheat the oven to 325 degrees F. Butter the bottom of a Bundt cake pan and sprinkle with the slivered almonds. In a mixing bowl, using an electric mixer, combine the cake and pudding mixes, water, rum, oil, and eggs and mix for 2 minutes. Pour into the Bundt pan and bake for 50 to 60 minutes, or until a toothpick comes out clean. Cool and remove from pan. Pour the warm glaze over the top of the cake.

To make the glaze: Mix all the ingredients in a saucepan and cook for about 2 minutes.

TWO-CRUST BANANA PIE

Serves 8

This type of banana pie is hardly ever made at home anymore. It is much more common to see banana cream or meringue pies done commercially. The two crusts make it similar to old-fashioned apple and berry pies.

2   9-inch pie crusts, unbaked
3   cups bananas, cut into slices
1   cup pineapple juice
$^1/_2$ cup sugar
3   tablespoons flour
1   teaspoon cinnamon
$^1/_2$ teaspoon nutmeg
    A pinch of salt
1   tablespoon butter
2   tablespoons milk

Make the double-crust pie crust on page 83. Preheat the oven to 400 degrees F. Soak bananas in the pineapple juice for 30 minutes. Drain. In a medium bowl, combine the sugar, flour, cinnamon, nutmeg, and salt and mix with bananas. Roll half the pie crust and place in the bottom of a 9-inch pie pan. Pour filling into pan on top of crust. Dot top of filling with butter. Place the rolled top crust over the filled pie. Seal and flute edges. Brush top with milk and cut slits for steam. Bake for 30 to 35 minutes. Serve warm or cold with vanilla ice cream.

SPRECKELS: THE ERA OF THE SUGAR KING

On August 24, 1876, Claus Spreckels sailed into Honolulu Harbor aboard the steamer *City of San Francisco*. Ironically, he was aboard the very ship bringing the news of the newly signed Reciprocity Treaty with the United States, promising the duty-free entry of sugar into the country.

Spreckels, an immigrant from a poor German family, had already made a fortune in California in sugar refining and had at first objected to the treaty. But being an opportunist of the first order, when he saw he couldn't stop its passage, he sought to profit from it.

His Hawaiian career was fraught with corruption and palace intrigue as well as tremendous financial success. As part of the powerful triumvirate made up of King Kalākaua, Walter Murray Gibson (an excommunicated Mormon missionary turned royal confidant), and himself, the sugar baron bought favors and influence and promoted economic development in the late nineteenth century as few had before or since.

When Kalākaua lay dying in San Francisco, Spreckels was one of the few at his bedside. When the monarchy fell in 1893, he fought to have it restored—not because he was a sentimental man, but because he thought it was good business. Contract labor was essential to the sugar industry, and he feared the U.S. government wasn't likely to go for its continuance.

Before Spreckels, much of what is now central Maui was "a great stretch of treeless plains . . . a poor windswept pasture, considered utterly unsuited for any kind of farming because there were no running streams."* Spreckles had acquired the land, but needed vast amounts of water. This he got in a questionable deal pulled off in the middle of the night, whereby he got water rights in East Maui in exchange for a loan to his old card-playing buddy, King Kalākaua.

It was the start of one of his biggest island accomplishments, the Spreckels Ditch. With German irrigation engineer Hermann Schussler, Spreckels built a ditch thirty miles long that delivered 60 million gallons of water a day to central Maui.

Alexander and Baldwin had already built the shorter Hāmākua Ditch, which was probably even more of an accomplishment because it was done without the expertise, or the money, of someone like Schussler. But Spreckels' ditch was bigger, and it transformed the central plain.

Spreckelsville plantation was successful in other ways as well. Spreckels built three sugar mills completed in 1882, was largely responsible for the development of the port at Kahului, and was the first to haul cane on a large scale by railroad. He installed electric lights in his mills five years before they were installed in 'Iolani Palace.

On several occasions Spreckels entertained the king, the widowed Queen Emma, and Princess Ruth by taking them on inspections of the mills before "music, wine, and cake" were served aboard one of the sugar trains.

Unfortunately, Spreckels bragged too loudly, and too often, about his influence over Kalākaua, and the increasingly tough terms of his loans to the kingdom led to his fall from grace.

He returned to California, and years later, in 1898, after a bitter family battle over the sugar interests, the Spreckelsville plantation (Hawaiian Commercial & Sugar Company) was taken over at a stockholders meeting. Alexander & Baldwin became the agent for the company in Honolulu.

In 1926, HC&S was incorporated in Hawai'i under the leadership of H. P. Baldwin and his son, F. F. Baldwin. The era of the Sugar King had finally ended.

* Source: Jacob Adler, *Claus Spreckels*, Honolulu: University of Hawai'i Press, 1966.

7

Rice and Noodles

Islanders are crazy about rice and noodles. At one time, these staples may have been prized because they were filling—and inexpensive. They were "poor people food." But no longer. Rice is the backbone, the mainstay, of any local plate lunch. Anything is a worthy meal when accompanied by steamed white rice. Rice balls with salty ume are tucked into bento lunches, two scoops beside macaroni salad is standard at lunch wagons. Sushi or a pan of dry noodles is a must at any gathering or buffet.

Enjoy these rice and noodle dishes at any time of the day or night—at any time of the year. They are island classics.

95

COLD SESAME NOODLES

Serves 8

This is a haole version of Chinese noodles. You can use any kind of leftover meat or char siu pork. It's a great way to clean out the refrigerator.

1	pound linguine
1/2	cup chopped watercress
4	tablespoons sesame oil
4	tablespoons shoyu
1/2	teaspoon minced garlic
	Freshly ground black pepper to taste
1/2	pound fresh snow peas, or 1 6-ounce package frozen snow peas, rinsed and thawed
	3 stalks green onion, chopped
	Toasted sesame seeds for garnish

Cook the linguine according to the package directions. But cook only until al dente, or still firm to the bite. Pour into a colander and rinse with cold water. In a large bowl, mix the watercress, sesame oil, shoyu, garlic, and black pepper. Add the noodles and toss. Cover and refrigerate overnight. In a steamer, cook the snow peas for 2 minutes. Add to the noodles and toss with the green onion. Serve chilled or at room temperature. Garnish with sesame seeds.

COUNTY FAIR CHOW FUN

Serves 6

A purist would insist on serving this in a cone-shaped paper cup with the shoyu sprinkled on top.

3/4	pound ground pork
2	teaspoons fresh ginger, chopped
4	tablespoons shoyu
1/2	teaspoon sugar
1	tablespoon oil
1	cup grated carrot
1	10-ounce package bean sprouts
1	cup chopped celery
1	tablespoon sesame oil
1	tablespoon oyster sauce
2	7-ounce packages chow fun noodles, or look fun noodles cut into 1/4-inch strips
1/2	cup green onion, chopped

In a bowl, mix the pork, 1 teaspoon ginger, 1 tablespoon shoyu, and 1/2 teaspoon sugar. Let stand for 15 minutes. In a large skillet, heat the oil and sauté the pork until browned. Add the grated carrot, then the bean sprouts and celery. Season with the sesame oil, oyster sauce, and 3 tablespoons of the shoyu. Add the noodles and toss to heat through. Add the green onion and stir-fry until everything is cooked and blended, about 1 minute.

CURRIED RICE SALAD

Serves 4

Any chicken-flavored rice will do for this dish. Peanuts and cashews can be added if you don't have macadamia nuts. This is a wonderful make-ahead dish for lunch or a potluck meal.

1   package chicken Rice-A-Roni mix
2   jars marinated artichoke hearts
1/4   teaspoon or more curry powder
1/3   cup mayonnaise
2   green onions, chopped, including some of the green tops
1/2   green or red bell pepper, chopped and seeded
8   green pimiento-stuffed olives, sliced
1   cup cooked chicken, diced (optional)
1/2   cup chopped macadamia nuts

Cook the Rice-A-Roni according to the package directions. Cool. Drain the artichokes, reserving the marinade. Make a dressing by combining the marinade with the curry powder and mayonnaise. Mix the dressing into the cooked rice mixture. Add the green onion, bell pepper, and olives and refrigerate 2 to 3 hours or overnight. Add chicken, nuts, and more mayonnaise before serving.

LAYERED PAN SUSHI

Serves 12 to 15

Pan sushi is a simple way to serve a crowd at potluck. This is one of many variations. Layer with your favorite Japanese pickles or condiments.

5   cups cooked white rice
1   can water-packed chunk tuna
1 1/2   tablespoons brown sugar
1   teaspoon shoyu
Salt to taste
1/2   cup Japanese rice vinegar
1/2   cup granulated sugar
1/4   cup shredded nori
1/4   cup furikake
1/4   cup shredded pickled ginger

Cook the rice in a rice cooker. In a saucepan over medium-high heat, combine the tuna, brown sugar, shoyu, and salt. In a bowl, mix together the vinegar, white sugar, and salt to taste. Scoop the hot rice into a large mixing bowl and fold the vinegar and sugar mixture into the rice to coat. Line a 9- x 13-inch pan with waxed paper. Sprinkle the bottom of the pan with the nori. Spread half the vinegared rice on top of the nori and press down. Spread the tuna mixture on top of the rice and sprinkle with furikake. Spread the rest of the rice on top of the tuna and press down. Sprinkle the pickled ginger on top. Keep refrigerated until ready to use. Serve from the pan, or cut into 2-inch squares.

GINGER UDON SALAD

Serves 4 to 6

Udon is a thick, starchy pasta found in the refrigerator cases of Asian groceries. It's most commonly eaten with piping hot broth, but it also makes a colorful marinated salad perfect for a buffet or picnic.

1	pound fresh udon noodles, cooked according to package directions

Dressing:

2	tablespoons canola oil
$1/2$	cup fresh lemon juice
$1/2$	cup sesame oil
$1/2$	cup shoyu
$1/2$	cup honey
2	tablespoons minced fresh ginger
1	clove minced garlic
	Freshly ground black pepper to taste

2	8-ounce cans sliced water chestnuts
2	cups chopped green onion, including green tops
$3/4$	cup finely diced red bell peppers
1	cup toasted slivered almonds
2	tablespoons black goma (sesame seeds), optional

In a pot of boiling water, cook the udon noodles for 6 minutes, or according to package directions. Drain in a colander and run under the cold water to rinse. Place in a salad bowl, cover, and refrigerate.

Add the water chestnuts, green onion, red peppers, and almonds to the noodles. Add dressing to taste and toss. Garnish with the sesame seeds. Chill well before serving.

To make the dressing: In a blender, combine the canola oil, lemon juice, sesame oil, shoyu, honey, ginger, garlic, and pepper. Mix.

PANCIT

Serves 6

Pancit is a popular Filipino noodle dish. Its basic difference from Chinese-style noodles is the addition of patis, or fish sauce, and the mixing of pancit noodles with long rice.

1	8-ounce package pancit, or chuka soba noodles
1	7.5-ounce package long rice (cellophane noodles)
2	tablespoons oil
2	cloves minced garlic
$1/2$	pound ground pork or chicken
1	medium carrot, cut into matchstick strips
$1/4$	head of cabbage, cut into small strips
$1/4$	pound dried 'ōpae (shrimp)
3	cups chicken broth
1	tablespoon oyster sauce
2	tablespoons patis (fish sauce)
	Salt and pepper to taste
5 to 6	dried shiitake mushrooms, reconstituted and sliced into strips
3	stalks green onion, chopped

Cook the pancit, or soba noodles, according to package directions, and drain (some kinds do not need to be cooked). Soak the long rice in warm water for about $1/2$ hour. Drain and cut long rice into 3-inch pieces. In a wok, heat the oil and sauté the garlic and ground pork or chicken. Add the carrots, cabbage, and dried shrimp. Stir-fry for about 2 minutes. Add the broth, oyster sauce, patis, salt, and pepper and bring to a boil. Add the long rice and mushrooms, then the noodles. Mix and stir-fry until everything is warm throughout and cooked. Garnish with green onion.

THE MAGIC OF MAILE

Open an office building and there is maile; graduate from high school, get married, or win a race for public office, and chances are you will be encircled by a strand of the fragrant, shiny leaves.

Maile is one of the oldest of the traditional Hawaiian lei. It is safe to say that the wearing of the vinelike shrub dates to the earliest settlers from Tahiti between the twelfth and fourteenth centuries. Maile lei, and the lei hala (pandanus), can be found throughout Polynesia.

The plant (Alyxia olivaeformis) grows in the forests of all islands on the middle and lower elevations. After the maile is gathered, the bark is pounded from the woody vine, leaving a stringy core in a process called ʻuʻu. Several strands are combined in the knotting method called kipuʻu, or a winding method called wili.

There are subtle differences in the maile from different islands, although much that is now used in Hawaiʻi is actually grown in the Cook Islands. Maile lau nui has large leaves; maile lau liʻi has smaller leaves, and maile liʻi liʻi has still smaller leaves. Other types are maile haʻi wale and maile kaluhea.

In the earliest of times and on into the early 1900s, lei took on special meanings, and some were reserved only for the aliʻi, or high born. One of the appeals of maile is that it has always been a lei for all the people.

Hawaiian gods often had parallels in nature, reflected in lei. For example, maile was the lei of Laka, the goddess of the hula, and offered at her altars. Pele, Laka's aunt, preferred the lei lehua, while Pele's sister Kukuena is associated with the lei ʻilima.

Legend has it that the demigod ʻAiwohikupua fell in love with the high chiefess Laʻieikawai. In the company of his maile sisters he wooed the chiefess but was turned down. Angry, he abandoned the maile sisters in the forest. The cleverest of the sisters befriended La'ieikawai and they, together with Kihanuilulumoku, the lizard, kept her safe from unsuitable lovers.

The Hawaiians used maile in their lovemaking and courtship in much the same way the French used perfume. It was also used after a battle as a symbol of peace.

Stories of festive events at 'Iolani Palace tell of decorating with maile, ginger, and pīkake early in the day and then closing the doors to retain the floral perfume. Just before the party began, the doors would be flung open and the guests assaulted by the sweet scents.

This oldest of traditional lei belongs in our lives and homes to this day. Wear maile, give maile, drape it in your homes for special events, and let the scent linger until it is dried. It is a powerful and spiritual statement of a Hawaiian heart.

Source: Marie A. McDonald, *Ka Lei: The Leis of Hawai'i*, Honolulu: Topgallant Publishing, 1978.

8

Verandas Remembered

For many of us born during the Territorial period (1900-1959), this chapter will be nostalgic. It was a time of steamship travel, long stays, and if you were lucky enough, gracious living on cool verandas that caught the trade winds on warm evenings.

For me, the memories are of trips to Honolulu and a stay at the old Alexander Young Hotel at the corner of Bishop and Hotel streets. The bakery downstairs was a favorite spot for palm leaves, English muffins, and their famous Lemon Crunch Cake.

In the early 1950s, our family took a bungalow in Waikīkī near the Ala Wai, and we kids snaked our way between the buildings, past the old Wagon Wheel Restaurant and the celebrity-studded Lau Yee Chai's, to the beach.

Lei sellers sold their wares at Honolulu's Aloha Tower and on the streets of Waikīkī. White linen and Panama hats with pheasant hatbands were the proper attire for gentlemen. Parades called for Hawaiian women to wrap themselves in pā'ū (riding attire) and gallop through town festooned with garlands of ginger, tuberose, and fragrant maile on Kamehameha Day.

103

The Moana Hotel bar was a place to spend an afternoon watching beach boys show visitors how to catch waves (and to watch the submarine races at night). Later, it was dinner and dancing at the Royal Hawaiian Hotel, or lobster with drawn butter and a floor show, complete with jewel-hued cellophane hula skirts, at the old Waikīkī Tavern.

I can still see my mother in a strapless black lace dress, her nails painted vermilion, and her big brown eyes bright in her beautiful hapa-haole face, as she kissed us all before bolting out the door with my father and their friends for a night on the town.

Peaches and Tony Guerrero ran the Tropics on Kalākaua Avenue in those days. And the best pancakes around were the gingerbread ones made piping hot each morning at Stewart's Pharmacy near Lewers Road.

These recipes may help you remember too.

AH MEE WONG'S CORNBREAD

Serves 9 to 10

This wonderful cornbread recipe belonged to Ah Mee Wong, who worked for the Shipman family of Hilo for fifty years. Ah Mee originally came to Shipman House to do yardwork, but within a very short time moved into the kitchen. Every morning he made his cornbread for the family. Whatever was left was cut into small squares and left outside the kitchen door as an after-school snack for the neighborhood children. The secret of this recipe is to heat the baking pan in the preheated oven before adding the batter. Doing this results in a very light cake. The recipe can be doubled and baked in a 9- x 14-inch pan for the same amount of time.

$^1/_2$	cup butter, softened
2	large eggs
$1^1/_2$	cups flour
1	heaping teaspoon baking powder
$^3/_4$	cup sugar
$^1/_4$	teaspoon salt
$1^1/_2$	tablespoons cornmeal
$^3/_4$	cup warm milk

Preheat the oven to 350 degrees F. In a large bowl, whisk together the softened butter and eggs. In a separate bowl, sift together the flour, baking powder, sugar, salt, and cornmeal. To the butter and egg mixture, add the warm milk. Blend well and then whisk in the dry ingredients. Mix well. There should be globs of butter in the mixture. Carefully pour the batter into a greased (use nonstick oil spray) 8- x 8-inch baking pan that has been heating in the oven. Bake 25 to 30 minutes. Turn oven off, but leave the cornbread in the hot oven a few more minutes to brown and crisp the top, if desired. Split pieces horizontally and spread with liliko'i butter or lehua honey.

CANLIS' SHRIMP SCAMPI

Serves 4

Canlis' Shrimp is good served with rice pilaf and a green salad. I think of it every time I pass the old building on Kalākaua Avenue near Saratoga Road.

3	tablespoons olive oil
28	large prawns, cleaned and shelled, with tails on
$1/4$	cup butter
2	garlic cloves, smashed
	Salt and freshly ground pepper to taste
$1/4$	cup dry vermouth
3	tablespoons lemon juice

Heat the olive oil in a large skillet over medium-high heat. When the oil is sizzling hot, sauté the shrimp quickly, reduce heat, and turn over. Add the butter, garlic, salt, and pepper. Just before the shrimp is done (it will turn pink), raise the heat to high and add the vermouth and lemon juice, constantly stirring and shaking the pan for no more than 1 minute. Do not overcook. Serve as an appetizer or entrée.

Chicken Laulau with Curry Sauce

Serves 6 to 8

Traditionally, laulau are made with lū'au leaves (the tops of the taro plant), butterfish, and salt pork, then wrapped in ti leaves and steamed. This version uses chicken breasts and thighs instead of the pork and fish, and substitutes fresh spinach for lū'au and cornhusks for ti leaves. The curry sauce is not Hawaiian. However, curry is very popular in Hawai'i, and a similiar dish was served in the Trader Vic's restaurants across the country in the 1950s. Trader Vic's ersatz Poly-Asian menu was part Cantonese, part Polynesian, and part Hollywood.

6	chicken breasts
6	chicken thighs
1/4	cup flour
	Salt and pepper to taste
2	tablespoons cooking oil
2	pounds fresh spinach leaves
1	large round onion, minced
	Hawaiian or kosher salt and pepper to taste
	Ti leaves or cornhusks, 2 per laulau
	String to tie

Dredge the chicken pieces in flour, salt, and pepper and brown on each side in oil. Drain on paper towels. Wash the spinach and wrap each piece of chicken and approximately 1 tablespoon minced onion with 5 or 6 leaves. Use more spinach if you like it. Cross 2 ti leaves and lay the spinach-wrapped chicken in the center. Fold like a package and tie with string, similiar to a tamale. Place the packages in a steamer with water in the bottom and steam slowly for 2 hours. Remove from the ti leaves and serve hot with curry sauce (see recipe, page 108).

CURRY SAUCE

Makes 3 cups

This curry sauce works as well over hard-cooked eggs and shrimp as with Chicken Laulau (see page 107). If fresh coconut is available, you can grate it yourself, add a quart of scalded milk to cover, and let it sit for an hour before straining through cheesecloth to make fresh coconut milk. The quicker way is to use the canned or frozen coconut milk available in most island grocery stores.

$1^1/_2$	tablespoons butter
1	medium round onion, finely chopped
1	clove garlic, minced
1	piece fresh ginger the size of a quarter, finely chopped
1 to 2	tablespoons Patak's curry paste or curry powder
$^1/_2$	teaspoon brown sugar
2	tablespoons flour
2	14-ounce cans coconut milk
$^1/_2$	cup chicken broth
	Salt to taste

In a saucepan over medium heat, melt the butter. Add chopped onion, garlic, and ginger and sauté until browned. Add curry paste or powder and sugar. Mix well. Add flour and stir. Gradually add the coconut milk, stirring constantly. If sauce is too thick, add the chicken broth to thin. Be sure not to cook on too high a heat or you will curdle the coconut milk. Add salt to taste.

Note: You may use the same condiments you would for a curry dinner.

HALEKŪLANI'S FAMOUS POPOVERS

Makes 6

There is no better way to enjoy a Waikīkī morning than to have these popovers, spread with pohā jam, while the surf laps gently on the beach near the House Without a Key at this landmark hotel.

2   cups milk
6   eggs
2   cups flour, sifted
1   teaspoon salt

Preheat the oven to 450 degrees F. Oil a large muffin tin and place it in the oven to heat. In a mixing bowl, combine the milk and eggs. With an electric mixer, combine until just blended. Sift together the flour and salt and add to the milk mixture, one half at a time, until blended. Remove the hot tins from the oven and fill $^3/_4$ full with the batter. Return tins to the oven and bake for 45 minutes, or until very brown. Serve with pohā jam.

KING KALĀKAUA'S CHAMPAGNE PUNCH

Serves 35 to 40

During the reign of King Kalākaua, a young lady named Marie von Holt was entertained at court. This recipe was passed down to her nephew, Herman von Holt, who held on to it. It was later published in a cookbook, Dining with the Daughters, *produced by the Daughters of Hawai'i. It stands the test of time and makes a wonderful punch for weddings or other festive occasions.*

6   bottles champagne
2   bottles sauterne
6   lemons, sliced in wheels
6   oranges, sliced in wheels
6   mint sprigs
1   ripe pineapple, sliced into spears
1   cup sugar
2   cups brandy
2   quarts fresh strawberries, hulled and halved

Chill the champagne and sauterne for 5 hours or overnight. Place a large block of ice in a large punchbowl and pour the chilled sauterne and 3 bottles of champagne over it. Add the sliced lemons and oranges, mint, pineapple, and sugar. Stir until sugar dissolves. Add the brandy and strawberries and stir gently. Immediately before serving, add the last 3 bottles of champagne.

KONA INN BANANA BREAD

Makes 2 loaves

The old Kona Inn sprawled out across a lawn fronting the bay at Kailua-Kona on the island of Hawai'i. During the 1940s and 1950s the bar was packed with hard-drinking and hard-living fishermen telling tales and watching as the sportfishing boats returned to the dock with their catches of marlin and 'ulua. In the morning, what they usually needed was a bit of the "hair of the dog" and breakfast served on the open lanai. This banana bread was a staple at breakfast or lunch and is as no-fail as you can get. It's also a great way to get rid of overripe bananas. Save one loaf to eat, and freeze the second for later.

2	cups sugar
1	cup softened butter (not margarine)
6	ripe bananas, mashed (approximately 3 cups)
4	eggs, well beaten
$2^1/_2$	cups cake flour
2	teaspoons baking soda
	1 teaspoon salt

Preheat oven to 350 degrees F. Cream together sugar and butter with an electric mixer until light and fluffy. Add bananas and eggs, beating until well mixed. Sift together dry ingredients 3 times. The 3 times is important. Don't skimp. Blend with banana mixture until just mixed. Don't over-mix. Pour into 2 lightly oiled 5- x 9- x 3-inch loaf pans. Bake for 45 minutes to 1 hour, until bread is firm in the center and the edges come away from the sides of the pans. Cool on wire racks. This bread freezes well.

CANLIS' MAHIMAHI CHOWDER

Serves 4 to 6

Mahimahi (dolphin family) is so wildly popular in Hawai'i because even people who don't ordinarily like fish enjoy its mild, sweet white meat. This chowder is a version of the one Larry Higashi, chef at the now defunct Canlis Restaurant in Waikīkī, used to make. If you don't have fresh mahimahi, any mildly flavored firm white fish will do. Evaporated skim milk can be substituted for the half and half, and skim milk for whole if you are watching fat.

4 to 5	slices chopped bacon		$1^1/_2$	quarts milk
1	large Maui onion, chopped		1	pint half and half
4	stalks celery, chopped		1	10-ounce can clam juice
2	large potatoes, peeled and cubed		2	cups water
1	green or red pepper, seeded and diced		4 to 5	drops Tabasco
	Salt and white pepper to taste		2	cups mahimahi, cooked (steamed or poached) and cubed
$1/_2$	tablespoon dried thyme			
1	tablespoon chicken bouillon			Chopped parsley for garnish
4	bay leaves			
$1^1/_4$	cups flour			

In a stockpot, over medium heat, sauté bacon until almost crisp. Add the onions and celery and cook in the bacon fat until they begin to soften. Add potatoes and green or red pepper and cook them until they begin to soften. Season with the salt, pepper, thyme, bouillon, bay leaves, and flour to make a roux. "Cook" the flour. (It will glump up a bit, but don't worry.) Slowly mix in the milk and half and half to make a thick soup. Keep stirring until mixture is smooth and cooked (mixture will not stick to the spoon). Continue to stir. In another saucepan, bring the clam juice and water to a boil and add slowly to the soup pot, stirring continually. Season with Tabasco. Bring mixture to a boil and add the mahimahi. Lower the heat and cook until the vegetables are done. Serve warm and garnish with chopped parsley.

THE WILLOWS GUAVA CAKE

Serves 10-12

When you're feeding a gang, this is the perfect cake. Make it to serve after Hawaiian food.

3 cups flour
2 tablespoons baking powder
$^1/_2$ teaspoon salt
$^1/_2$ pound butter, softened
$1^1/_2$ cups sugar
3 eggs
1 cup guava juice

Preheat the oven to 350 degrees F. Sift together the flour, baking powder, and salt. Beat the butter and sugar until creamy. Add the eggs to the butter and sugar until incorporated. Add the flour mixture to the butter mixture. Add the guava juice. Do not overmix. Grease a 9- x 12-inch baking pan and pour the batter into it. Bake for 25 to 30 minutes, or until the cake pulls away from the sides and the center springs back when touched. Cool and serve with whipped cream.

CRISPY HAUPIA

10 pieces of haupia, $1^1/_2$ inches square (see page 84)

1 egg white, beaten lightly
$^3/_4$ cup panko breadcrumbs
Oil for deep frying

Make the haupia according to the recipe on page 84. Cut into squares when firm. Dip each piece of haupia into the egg white, then into the panko to coat. Heat the oil in a deep skillet. Gently and quickly fry the breaded haupia in the oil until brown and crisp on the outside. Drain on paper towels. Serve warm with the curry (see page 113).

The Willows Shrimp Curry with Panko-Crisp Haupia

Serves 6

Hawai'i hostesses of earlier generations were famous for their curry dinner parties. The shrimp curry recipe here is from the much missed Willows Restaurant in Honolulu. It's a typically Hawaiian curry, and you can use chicken in place of shrimp. This curry changed slightly with each new chef and the tastes of the times. One of the best-known chefs was Kusuma Cooray, from Sri Lanka, who had previously cooked for Doris Duke at her Diamond Head home. She tweaked the curry up a notch. The Willows also made a wonderful version of haupia, which was served warm on the side. The haupia was dipped in panko crumbs and deep fried (see page 112).

Curry Sauce:

3	cloves garlic, minced
1/4	cup chopped fresh ginger
1	cup finely chopped onions
3	tablespoons unsalted butter
	Salt to taste
2	teaspoons sugar
3	tablespoons curry powder
4	tablespoons flour
1 to 2	quarts coconut milk, according to taste (Hawaiian style)

4	cups medium shrimp, uncooked
3/4	cup white wine
3	tablespoons peanut oil
	Salt and white pepper to taste
6	tablespoons curry powder

Peel the shrimp and cut in half lengthwise. Devein and wash. Marinate in white wine and 1 tablespoon peanut oil with salt and white pepper to taste. Let stand for 15 minutes. In a saucepan, heat 2 tablespoons of oil and sauté the 6 tablespoons of curry powder to release flavors. Add the marinated shrimp and cook until they just turn pink. Do not overcook. Add the sauce and heat through. Ladle over hot white rice. This is wonderful served with pan-fried bananas sprinkled with cinnamon, or guava jam, mango chutney, bacon bits, chopped green onion, macadamia nuts, and raisins.

To make the sauce: In a saucepan over medium heat, sauté the garlic, ginger, and onion in the butter. Add the salt, sugar, curry powder, and flour and brown lightly. Add the coconut milk a little at a time, stirring constantly. Continue to cook on medium-low heat for 20 minutes, or until the sauce is ready to boil. Remove from heat and cool.

REMEMBERING THE POI SUPPER

Until the early 1970s, when we all got a little more worldly and chic with our eating habits (and our attire), it was quite normal in Hawai'i to be invited to the houses of friends and relatives for laulau and poi on a Sunday night. Women wore mu'umu'u out to cocktail parties and dinner more regularly, and things in general were—well, more Hawaiian.

Poi suppers could be simple—or very elegant—occasions. Simple meant stopping by the local market and picking up laulau, lomi salmon, poi, Maui onions, limu, kālua pig, and whatever else looked good.

Elegant poi suppers, on the other hand, meant setting the table with your best linen, and if you were lucky, a special set of bowls and dishes (often coconut or native woods) made just for this sort of affair. Women dressed in holokū, with their long trains caught up at their wrists. They wore fresh ginger lei, and tucked gardenias and hibiscus into their hair. In retrospect, it all seems very romantic.

If you're looking for a new way to entertain with a touch of nostalgia—a way that will give your home a sense of place—why not throw a poi supper for friends? Buy some of the food, and make the rest. You

will have a very good time. Maybe you can even get some kama'āina to come up with an old bottle of 'ōkolehao.

Here are some ideas for dinner. The 'Ōpakapaka Laulau is an updated, more trendy version of the traditional laulau (or just pick up the chicken kind in the market). The other recipes are from the collection of Maili Yardley, cookbook author and longtime columnist for the *Honolulu Advertiser*, who is the absolute expert in this field.

'ŌPAKAPAKA LAULAU

Serves 4

Filling:

1/4	cup peanut oil
1	cup finely sliced Maui onions
1	cup minced garlic
3	cups shiitake mushrooms, julienned
1	teaspoon chili pepper water
1	teaspoon finely chopped fresh ginger
	Salt and white pepper to taste
1/3	cup finely chopped Chinese parsley (cilantro)
1/3	cup chopped green onion

Marinade:

2	tablespoons fish sauce (patis)
2	tablespoons shoyu
2	tablespoons peanut oil
1 1/2	pounds 'ōpakapaka, cut into 2-ounce pieces
8	ti leaves, washed and ribbed
1	cup of limu, or ogo (seaweed)

Make the filling by heating the peanut oil in a pan and sautéing the onions until clear. Add the garlic, mushrooms, chili pepper water, ginger, salt, and white pepper and continue to cook for 5 minutes. When cooked, add the Chinese parsley and green onion and set aside.

Prepare the marinade by mixing the fish sauce, shoyu, and peanut oil together. Coat the pieces of fish with the sauce and marinate for 30 minutes in the refrigerator. Do not add salt.

Wash the ti leaves and heat a pot of boiling water. Dip the stems into the hot water to soften and remove the tough rib with a knife, keeping the leaf whole. Take 2 leaves and make a cross. Cut the stem off one of the leaves. Spoon 1/4 of the filling into the center of the leaves. Place a piece of fish and some ogo on top of the filling. Close the leaves, making a bundle: wrap the leaf without the stem around the filling first; then take the other leaf and wrap it around and under the stem to make a knot. (If all else fails, use string.) Steam the laulau for 10 to 15 minutes in a steamer on top of the stove.

CRAB LŪʻAU BAKE

Serves 6

2 cups chopped lūʻau leaves, cooked (can use the frozen leaves)

2 cups crabmeat

1 cup sour cream

$^1/_2$ cup mayonnaise

Salt to taste

2 cups crushed garlic croutons

$^1/_3$ cup melted butter

Preheat the oven to 300 degrees F. If you use fresh lūʻau leaves, cook them in a pot of boiling water, changing the water at least once and repeating with fresh. You can also use frozen lūʻau leaves or frozen whole-leaf spinach. The lūʻau leaves will wilt and cook in the same way as spinach. Drain and cool. In a bowl, mix the crabmeat, sour cream, mayonnaise, and salt. Add the cooked lūʻau and mix well. Spread the mixture in a 2-quart casserole dish and top with the crushed croutons. Pour the melted butter over the top and bake for 1 hour.

GUAVA-GLAZED SWEET POTATOES

Serves 8

8   medium sweet potatoes, cooked (or a 17-ounce can of sweet potatoes)
1   cup guava jelly
2   tablespoons butter

Cook the sweet potatoes in a large pot of boiling water until done. Cool, peel, and cut them in half, or into good serving sizes. Arrange the potatoes in a greased baking dish. Heat the jelly and butter in a saucepan until they make a syrup and heat through. Drizzle the syrup over the potatoes. Bake at 300 degrees F. for 30 minutes, turning every 15 minutes or so to baste and glaze.

CHILI PEPPER WATER

Makes 3 cups

$2\frac{1}{2}$ cups boiling water
$\frac{3}{4}$ cup cold water
2   tablespoons white vinegar
1   clove garlic, minced
1   tablespoon chopped fresh ginger
14   or so small red Hawaiian chili peppers

Combine all the ingredients in a blender and process until smooth, about 30 seconds. Pour into sterilized bottles, cover, and refrigerate. Sterilize your bottles by washing and submerging them in a large pot filled with water. (Make sure the bottles fill with water.) Cover and bring to a boil. Cook for at least 10 minutes. Leave the lid on the pot and allow the water to return to room temperature. With a pair of tongs, remove the bottles and caps to drain and air dry. Do not wipe with a cloth.

THE ALOHA SHIRT

In 1936 a Honolulu shirtmaker named Ellery J. Chun began making a shirt of brightly colored fabric meant to be worn outside the trousers. He named his creation the "aloha shirt." Chun's shirts sold for a dollar in his store near the corner of King and Smith streets.

The real origins of the aloha shirt go back even farther, however, to a garment called the "Thousand Mile Shirt," worn by early pioneers crossing the United States on their way to Oregon and California in the nineteenth century.

This shirt was sturdy and durable—and meant to be worn as a smock. The shirt found its way to Hawai'i because of the extensive travel by sailing ships between Hawai'i and the West Coast. Soon Chinese and Japanese immigrants were producing it, often in denim and palaka, to wear as work clothes on Hawai'i plantations.

Two factors created the early aloha shirt. The first was the growing tourism industry centered at Waikīkī Beach around the Royal Hawaiian, Moana, and Halekūlani hotels.

The new tourists wanted souvenirs to take home and cool, comfortable clothing to wear while they vacationed. Soon Waikīkī fashion leaders such as Elsie Das and Musa-Shiya were producing custom versions for this market. Custom shirts were a status symbol and were often produced especially for an event such as a party, anniversary, or wedding.

The second factor was the creation in 1924 by the DuPont Company of a miracle fabric called "rayon." Rayon was a synthetic fabric made from cellulose and natural wood pulp. Previous aloha shirts had been made mostly of silk or cotton, but rayon made them cheaper to produce and held the brilliant dyes better.

By the 1930s, aloha shirts were being mass produced by two pioneers—Kamehameha Garment Co. and Branfleet (which later became Kāhala).

Fabric was designed in Hawai'i, printed in California, and manufactured back in Hawai'i. Between 1936 and 1939 the Hawaiian garment industry "took off." Kāhala even managed to get Hawai'i's most well known athlete, Duke Kahanamoku, to endorse their product for a small royalty.

World War II caused a slowdown in garment production, but it brought thousands of U.S. servicemen to Hawai'i, and many of them wanted to return after the war. In 1948, Aloha Week was founded, and tourism again took off—and along with it, the craze for the aloha shirt.

Designers such as Shaheen's and Paradise Sportswear joined the early manufacturers of shirts and added women's lines as well. The shirts of this period are valued for their workmanship (pockets often match the design on the body of the shirt), coconut buttons, and unique patterns. In the early 1950s the DuPont factory burned down, and with it, the specific quality of rayon they produced was lost.

Collectors look for rare designs and color combinations of aloha shirts, also called "silkies." Some of the earliest shirts had metal buttons with the Royal Hawaiian crest.

Among the labels produced in Hawai'i and California are Surfriders Sportswear, Paradise Hawai'i, Watumull's, 'Iolani, Russell's, Olu-Olu, McInerny's, Ross Sutherland, Malihini, Shaheen's, and of course, Kamehameha and Kāhala.

Source: H. Thomas Steele, *The Hawaiian Shirt,* New York: Abbeville Press, 1984.

Photo Credits

Photos by or from the personal collection of Kaui Philpotts: front cover, pages iii, iv, v, vii, 1, 3, 4, 5, 7, 8-9, 10, 11, 13, 14, 20, 22, 26-27, 28, 38, 42-43, 47, 50, 53, 58-59, 65, 67, 68-69, 70, 78-79, 80, 84, 89, 91, 94-95, 99, 102-103, 104, 114

Hawaii State Archives: pages 25, 40, 56-57, 77, 93, 101

Burl Burlington AirChive: page 119

Honolulu Academy of Arts (#5803.1). 'Ulu (Breadfruit). Maker unknown. Hawaiian Islands, circa 1930. Plain cotton, hand appliqué, contour quilting, and machine stitched edging; 84 in. (213.4 cm) x 86 in. (218.5 cm). Gift of Rosalie Young Persons, 1986: page 41

Carol Austin: author photo, back flap

GLOSSARY OF INGREDIENTS

'ahi — The Hawaiian name for both yellowfin and bigeye tuna. Often consumed in the islands as sashimi (Japanese-style raw fish).

aku — The Hawaiian name for skipjack tuna. Deep red in color and stronger-tasting than 'ahi. Good broiled or grilled, or used raw in poke.

a'u — The Hawaiian name for swordfish, or marlin.

bagoong — Strong-flavored fermented Filipino fish sauce.

bamboo shoots — Young, cone-shaped shoots sold fresh or in cans in Asian markets.

bean sprouts — Mung beans that have sprouted. Available fresh or canned.

bean thread noodles — Also called cellophane noodles, glass noodles, or long rice. Purchase dry and reconstitute in water before using.

breadfruit — A bland, starchy vegetable widely used in the Pacific, but difficult to get on the U.S. mainland. Potatoes are a good substitute.

cellophone noodles — Also called bean thread noodles, glass noodles, or long rice. Purchase dry and reconstitute in water before using.

char siu — Pork or beef that has been marinated in a sweet-spicy red sauce and dried. Used in small amounts to flavor noodle dishes or as a side dish.

chili paste — A thick chili paste used in many Asian cuisines, such as Thai, Vietnamese, Indonesian, and Filipino. The sauce is made of chilis, onions, sugar, and tamarind.

chili pepper water — A hot mixture of small red chilies, salt, vinegar, and garlic. See the recipe on page 117.

Chinese cabbage — A crinkled leaf cabbage also called won bok or napa cabbage.

Chinese Five Spice — A spice mixture of anise, cinnamon, cloves, fennel, and star anise. Available already mixed in Asian markets.

Chinese long rice	Also called bean thread noodles, cellophone noodles, or glass noodles. Purchase dry and reconstitute in water before using.
Chinese parsley	Also known as cilantro.
coconut	The edible nut of the coconut tree. Most commonly used is the coconut milk, which is extracted from the shredded "meat" by straining it with hot water. (This is not the drinkable coconut water in the coconut's center.)
daikon	Japanese name for a white, crisp radish-type root vegetable. Turnips can be substituted.
dau see	Black bean sauce.
fish sauce	Called nam pla in Thai cuisine or nuoc mam in Vietnamese cuisine. Very salty and pungent. Made from fermented small fish and shrimp. Available in Asian markets.
furikake	A spicy Japanese seaweed seasoning mix.
gari shoga	Pickled ginger.
ginger	Fresh ginger is a brown, fibrous, knobby rhizome. It keeps for long periods of time. To use, peel the brown outside skin and slice, chop, or purée for use in many dishes. It will keep indefinitely if peeled and placed in a jar with sherry. Store in the refrigerator.
glass noodles	Also called bean thread noodles, cellophone noodles, or long rice. Purchase dry and reconstitute in water before using.
goma	Black sesame seeds available packaged or bottled in Japanese markets.
green papaya	Green fruit usually shredded and used in salads and stir-frys in Southeast Asian cuisines.
guava	A round, tropical fruit with yellow skin and pink inner flesh. Grown commercially in Hawai'i. The purée or juice is available as a frozen concentrate. You can also find it in jams, jellies, and sauces.

haupia	Traditional Hawaiian pudding made of coconut milk, sugar, and cornstarch.
Hawaiian chili pepper	Small, very spicy red chili pepper.
Hawaiian salt	A coarse sea salt that often collects at the water's edge in tidal pools after a storm or high tide. The salt is gathered gingerly and put into burlap bags to be dried further and stored. Hawaiians sometimes mixed it with a red clay ('alaea salt) Substitute kosher salt.
hoisin sauce	A thick, brownish, garlicky, and sweet sauce made from soybean paste, sugar, and spices. Can be purchased bottled.
hondashi	Japanese stock seasoning, used for broths.
imu	A firepit or underground oven used in Hawaiian cooking, in which hot volcanic stones are used to steam food.
Japanese eggplant	A purple, enlongated variety of eggplant. Substitute the round kind unless recipe specifies otherwise.
Japanese plum wine	Made from the Japanese plum, or ume, and available in Asian and specialty markets.
kajiki	The Japanese name for Pacific blue marlin. Substitute swordfish or shark.
kalo	The Hawaiian name for the taro root, or corm.
kālua pig	Smoky, shredded pork that has been cooked in a traditional underground pit, or imu.
kiawe	Also known as mesquite. An excellent charcoal is made from the wood of the kiawe tree.
laulau	A bundle of meat, fish, and taro leaves (lū'au) wrapped in ti leaves and steamed. A traditional Hawaiian dish.
liliko'i	The Hawaiian name for passion fruit. Substitute orange juice if the purée is not available.

limu	Hawaiians gather as many as twenty-five varieties of seaweed (e.g., limu līpoa, limu kohu, limu ʻeleʻele). Japanese ogo is a type of limu. Much of the ogo today is farm-raised.
lomi lomi salmon	A fresh-tasting Hawaiian salad of salt-cured salmon (rinsed), onion, and tomato.
long rice	Also called bean thread noodles, cellophone noodles, or glass noodles. Purchase dry and reconstitute in water before using.
lūʻau	A traditional Hawaiian feast that usually includes foods prepared in an imu, or underground oven. Kālua pig, laulau, sweet potato, chicken lūʻau, lomi lomi salmon, and haupia are almost always served.
lūʻau leaves	Young, green taro tops. Substitute fresh spinach.
lychee	A small fruit with white meat and a hard shell that bears fruit during the summer months. Available in Asian markets. The canned version is a good substitute.
macadamia nut oil	A premium cooking and salad oil produced in Hawaiʻi from macadamia nuts. Has a particularly high heat threshold for burning.
macadamia nuts	A rich, oily nut grown mostly on the Big Island of Hawaiʻi. Native to Australia.
mahimahi	Dolphinfish with firm, pink flesh. Best fresh, but often available frozen. Substitute snapper, catfish, halibut.
mango	Golden and green tropical fruit available anywhere you can buy exotic fruit. Available fresh June through September in Hawaiʻi. Substitute fresh peaches.
Maui onion	A very sweet, juicy, large round onion similiar to Vidalia or Walla Walla onion. Can often be found on the West Coast.
miso	A soybean paste made by salting and fermenting soybeans and rice. Shiro miso, or white miso, is the mildest of several different types. Purchase in Asian markets. Can be stored for months in the refrigerator.

mochiko sweet rice flour	Japanese glutinous rice flour used in making pastries and some sauces.
napa cabbage	Also known as Chinese cabbage or won bok.
nori	Sheets of dried and compressed seaweed used in making rolled sushi. Available in Japanese markets.
ogo	Japanese name for seaweed, or limu.
onaga	Japanese name for red snapper. Best steamed, baked, or sautéed. Substitute monkfish or orange roughy.
'ono	A mackerel with white, firm flesh. Also known as wahoo. Substitute tuna, swordfish, or shark.
opah	A very large moonfish. Substitute swordfish.
'ōpakapaka	A pink snapper with delicate flavor. Works best poached, baked, or sautéed. Substitutes are any snapper, sea bass, or monkfish.
'opihi	A small limpet gathered from the rocks along the coastline. Most often eaten raw, and sometimes grilled. Similar to a snail in texture and an oyster in flavor. Because 'opihi are difficult to gather, they are considered a delicacy.
oyster sauce	A concentrated sauce made from oyster juice and salt. Used in many Chinese and other Asian dishes. Will keep a long time in the refrigerator.
panko	Crispy, large-flaked Japanese breadcrumbs. They add more texture than ordinary breadcrumbs. Found in Asian markets.
papaya	A small tropical fruit with a yellow flesh, black seeds, and a perfumey scent. Also see green papaya.
passion fruit juice concentrate	Also known as liliko'i juice concentrate. Can be found in the frozen juice section of markets. Substitute orange juice concentrate.
patis fish sauce	A strong-flavored and -smelling seasoning sauce used in Southeast Asian cuisines. Tiparos is one brand name.

pickled ginger	A bottled, pickled version of ginger. Usually preserved in rice wine vinegar.
pipikaula	The Hawaiian version of beef jerky, often made with venison.
plum sauce	Also called Chinese plum sauce. A sweet-and-sour sauce available in most Asian markets.
plum wine	See Japanese plum wine.
pohā	Hawaiian name for cape gooseberries.
poi	A starchy paste made by pounding the root of the taro plant with water until it reaches a smooth consistency. A staple in the traditional Hawaiian diet.
poke	A traditional Hawaiian raw fish dish made with fish such as aku or 'ahi, chili peppers, seaweed, Hawaiian salt, and kukui nuts. The contemporary poke often has sesame oil, shoyu, and green onion.
Portuguese sausage	A pork sausage with lots of small red chili peppers. Substitute hot Italian sausages.
pupus	Appetizers.
rice wine vinegar	A light vinegar made from fermented rice.
sake	Japanese rice wine.
sesame seeds	Small white or black (goma) seeds used to flavor or garnish main dishes and desserts.
sesame oil	A strong-flavored oil made from sesame seeds and used in most Asian cuisines. Only a small amount is needed for flavoring. Sesame oil burns at a lower heat than most oils. Refrigerate after opening.
shiitake mushrooms	Available fresh or dried in Asian markets. To reconstitute the dried variety, soak in water before using. Do not use the dried stems.
shoyu	The Japanese and local Hawaiian name for soy sauce.

shutome	The name for the Hawaiian broadbill swordfish. Has a high fat content. Substitute any swordfish.
snow peas	Peas with edible pods, often used in stir-fry dishes.
soba noodles	Thin and brown, soba noodles are made from buckwheat and wheat flour. They cook quickly and can be served hot or cold.
soy sauce	Often called in Hawai'i by its Japanese name, shoyu. A dark salty liquid made from soybeans, flour, salt, and water. A staple in most Asian cuisines. Sweet soy sauce is called kecap manis in Indonesian cooking.
star anise	Brownish seeds with eight points. They taste like licorice.
tako	The Japanese name for octopus. A popular appetizer when prepared as poke or smoked.
tamarind	Brown, bean-shaped pod from the tamarind tree. The fruit tastes sweet-sour. Made into sauces, candy, pastes.
taro	The starchy vegetable that is turned into the traditional Hawaiian staple, poi. Also used in Chinese and other Asian dishes.
taro leaves	Also called lū'au leaves. The leafy green tops of the taro plant. Substitute fresh spinach.
ti leaves	The smooth leaves of the ti plant. Used to steam and bake fish and vegetables. Often called the "Hawaiian aluminum foil."
Tiparos fish sauce	A brand of bottled Filipino fish sauce used to season many Asian dishes.
tofu	Soybean curd. Has a soft, mild flavor. Can be purchased fresh in Asian markets.
venison	Deer meat. Island venison is hunted primarily on the islands of Lāna'i, Moloka'i, and Hawai'i. Because it has so little fat, venison is usually marinated or cooked slowly in liquid. Venison is a favorite meat for pipikaula, a version of beef jerky.
wakame	Dried seaweed that is reconstituted and used in Japanese dishes.
won bok	Cabbage-like vegetable also called napa or Chinese cabbage.

Recipe Index

129

Notes

Notes

Notes

Notes